W9-CQQ-939

Communication Arts

2002
Illustration
Annual

Volume 44, Number 3
www.commarts.com

COMMUNICATION ARTS,
(ISSN 0010-3519) is published eight
times a year (January/February,
March/April, May/June, July Illustration
Annual, August Photography Annual,
September/October Interactive Design
Annual, November Design Annual
and December Advertising Annual)
by Coyne & Blanchard, Inc., 110
Constitution Drive, Menlo Park, CA
94025-1107.

Periodicals postage paid at Menlo
Park, CA and at additional mailing
offices.

SUBSCRIBER SERVICES:
Subscription: 1 year, $53; in Canada,
$70; All other countries, $110. All
payment in U.S. dollars, Canadian
GST: 127848620. Direct all inquiries,
address changes, subscription
orders, etc., to:

COMMUNICATION ARTS
P.O. Box 51785, Boulder, CO, 80322-
1785. Via phone: 800-688-1971;
303-678-8475; fax: 303-661-1181 or
e-mail: subscription@commarts.com.
Please allow six weeks for changes.
For back issues, please contact the
editorial and business office.

EDITORIAL AND BUSINESS OFFICE:
110 Constitution Drive, Menlo Park,
CA 94025-1107. Phone: 650-326-6040;
fax: 650-326-1648; e-mail:
ca@commarts.com.

POSTMASTER: Send changes
of address to:

COMMUNICATION ARTS
P.O. Box 51785
Boulder, CO 80328-1785

 ABC

Cover Illustration © 2002 Nicholas Wilton
One from a series portraying aliens. Mark Murphy, art director;
Murphy Design, design firm. 8 × 8, acrylic on cement block.

Communication Arts

2002
Illustration
Annual

43

July 2002
Volume 44, Number 3

categories

fresh

columns

departments

Editor and Designer
Patrick Coyne

Executive Editor
Jean A. Coyne

Managing Editor
Anne Telford

Associate Editor
Rebecca Bedrossian

Associate Designer
Mark Eastman

Production Manager
Scott Perry

Production
Ron Niewald

Technology Director
Jeff Stafford

Interactive Media Art Director
Bonnie Smetts

Interactive Media Designer
Tricia Seibold

Interactive Media Editor
Sue Garibaldi

Interactive Media Programmer
Duncan Brown

Interactive Media Developer
Gary Wium

Interactive Media Producer
Becky Fong

Interactive Media Production Assistant
Khader Yanni

Information Systems Manager
Michael Hoyt

Web Administrator
Nancy Hagemann

General Manager Advertising/Circulation
Michael Krigel

Circulation Director
Perry Fotos

Retail Sales Manager
Gloria Rosario

Subscriptions
Priscilla Brooks
Michelle Estrin

Office Manager
Nina Kitching

Administration
Darcie Niewald

Controller
Ron Auger, CPA

Assistant Controller
Gayle Gregorius

Contributing Editors
Tad Crawford, Legal Affairs;
Barbara Gordon/Maria Piscopo, Freelance; DK Holland, Design Issues; Wendy Richmond, Design Culture; Ernie Schenck, Advertising

Founder
Richard Coyne (1926–1990)

Advertising

1 Jim Tsinganos, illustrator
Marco Cicchianni, art director
Lisa Mandic, designer
Advertising Designers Group, ad agency
Amnesty International, client

Poster celebrating 40 years of the formation of Amnesty
International. 11½ × 15, pastel.

2 Rob Day, illustrator
Kenny Patrick/Sloan Cooper, art directors
Alan Wolstencroft, writer/creative group head
Michael Thompson, creative director
Thompson & Company, ad agency
First Tennessee Bank, client

Outdoor board. 4 × 4.

3 Cynthia von Buhler, illustrator
Michele Locatelli, art director
Seattle Opera, client

CD cover for Seattle Opera's 2002/2003 season. 42 × 42,
gouache on canvas with a live dove, plaster and old keys.

4 Von R. Glitschka, illustrator/art director/designer
Glitschka Studios, design firm
Innsbrook Foundation for Cystic Fibrosis, client

Fundraiser CD cover. 4¾ × 4¾ digital.

5 Gary Baseman, illustrator
Ken Baker, art director/creative director
Momentum Saint Louis East, ad agency
Budweiser, client

Poster. Acrylic on canvas.

6 Gary Taxali, illustrator
John Locke, art director
Bonny Doon Vineyard, client

Wine label. 6¾ × 7¾, mixed media.

Advertising

1 (series)
Chris Valencius, illustrator
Marc Gallucci, art director
Fort Franklin, ad agency
Timberland, client

Series of three ads. 8 × 8, acrylic.

2 **Christian Clayton, illustrator**
Joe Sibb/Dickie Barrett, art directors
Side One Records, client

CD cover for The Mighty Mighty Bosstones.
14 × 14, mixed media on wood.

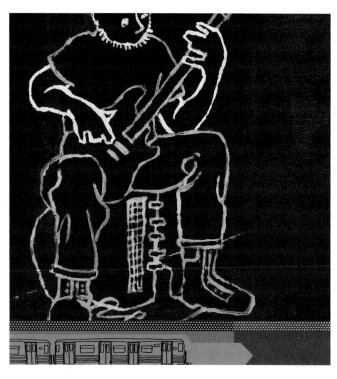

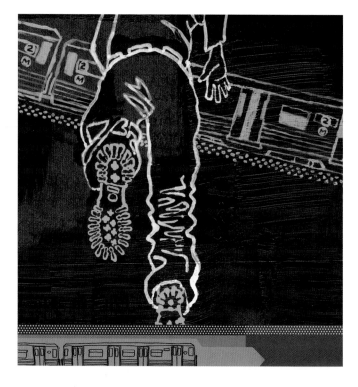

2

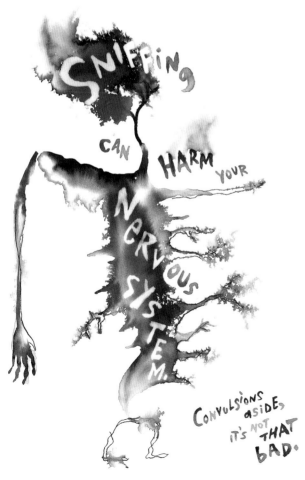

Advertising

1 Chris Gall, illustrator
   James Seacat, art director
   Actors Theatre of Louisville, client

   Poster. 12 × 16, scratchboard, digital.

2 (series)
   Paul Dallas, illustrator
   Bart Cleveland, art director
   Sawyer Riley Compton, ad agency
   Partnership for a Drug-Free America, client

   Three ads from a print campaign. 15 × 20, watercolor.

Advertising

1 Gary Baseman, illustrator
Rob Semos, art director
St. John & Partners, ad agency
Jacksonville Public Library, client

Poster for a book festival. Acrylic on canvas.

2 (series)
Traci Daberko/Dennis Clouse, illustrators/designers
Chad Bollenbach, art director
Cyclone Design, design firm
Lindsay Stone & Briggs, ad agency
Madison Repertory Theatre, client

Posters. Mixed media.

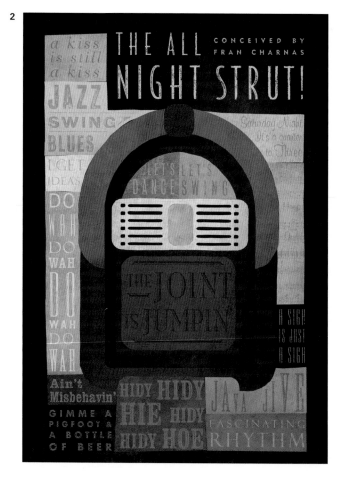

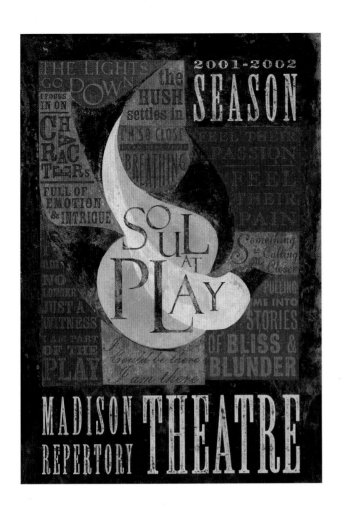

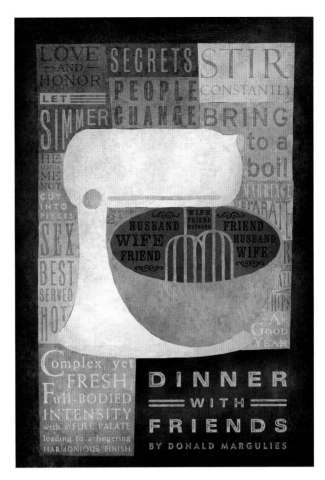

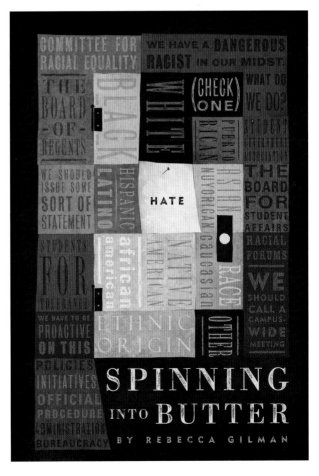

Advertising

1　Pierre Pratt, illustrator/art director/designer
　La Maison Théâtre, client

　Poster for children's theater. 10 × 16½, acrylic.

2　(series)
　José Luis Merino, illustrator
　Base Design, design firm
　Kid's Fashion Brussels, client

　Ads for children's fashion fair. Various sizes, mixed media.

Advertising

1 **Craig Frazier, illustrator/designer**
Craig Frazier/Russell Brown, art directors
Adobe, client

Poster for "Everywhere you Look" campaign. 8½ × 11, cut paper/digital.

2 **(series)**
Michael Hahn, illustrator/art director/designer
Nordharzer Städtebundtheater Halberstadt, client

Posters. 19½ × 27½, ink and Photoshop.

1

2

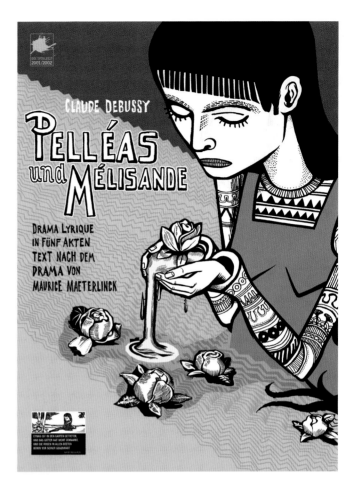

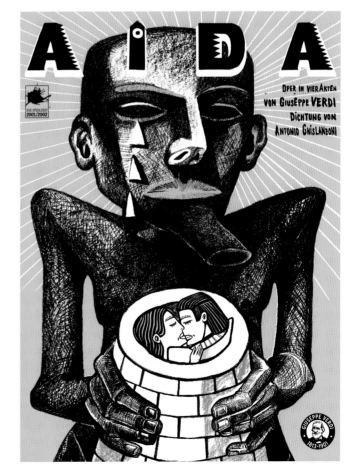

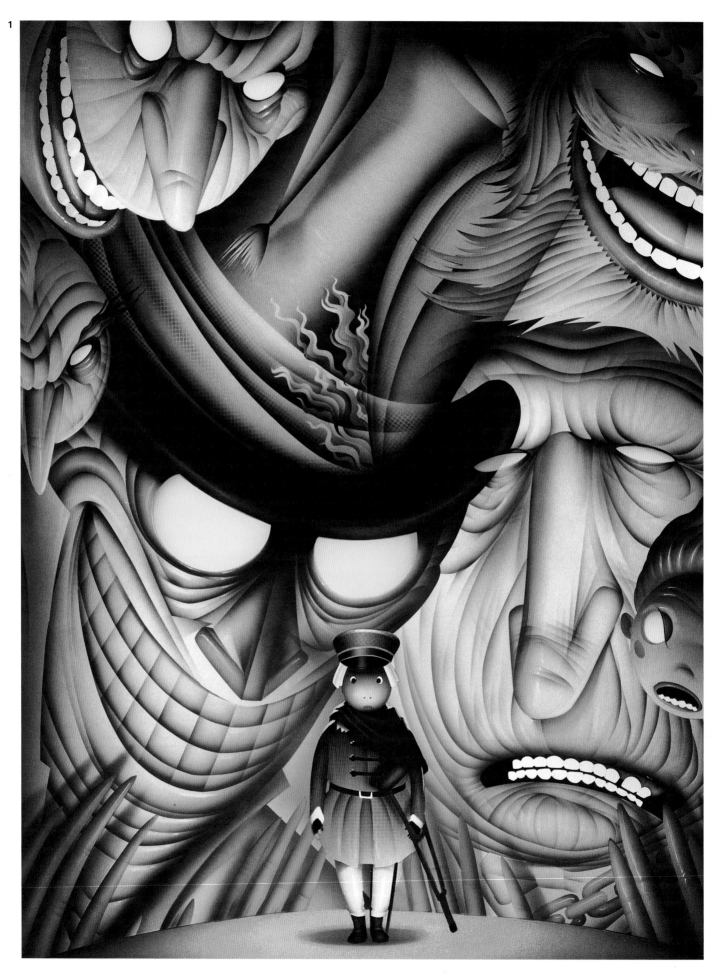

Advertising

1 (series)
Bill Mayer, illustrator
Harry Hartofelis, art director/designer
Hartford Stage, client

Series of posters used for local ads, brochures and programs.
15 × 20, airbrush, gouache and digital.

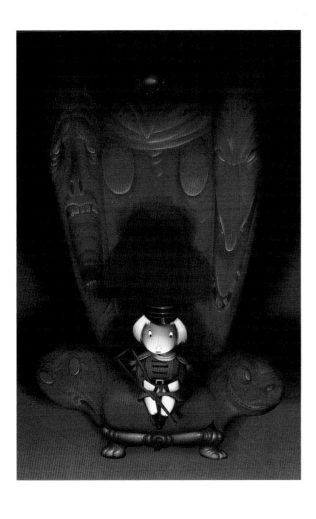

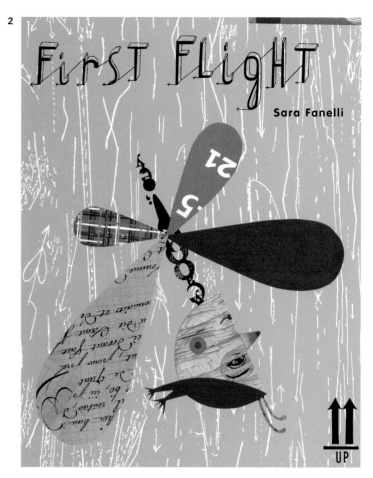

Books

1 Peter de Sève, illustrator
Rosanne Serra, art director
Penguin Putnam, client

Cover for *Treasury of Royal Scandals* by
Michael Farquhar. Watercolor and ink.

2 (series)
Sara Fanelli, illustrator
Chris Bigg, typographer
Jonathan Cape, Random House Children's
	Books, client

Cover and four spreads from *First Flight*
written and illustrated by Sara Fanelli.
Various sizes, collage.

Books

1 Daniel Adel, illustrator
   Denise Cronin, art director
   Penguin Putnam/Starbright Foundation, clients

   Rumpelstiltskin from *Once upon a Fairy Tale* children's book. 16 × 20, oil on canvas.

2 (series)
   Nicoletta Ceccoli, illustrator
   Fernando Ambrosi, art director
   Arnoldo Mondadori Editore, publisher/client

   Interior illustrations from *Le Avventure di Pinocchio* by Carlo Collodi.

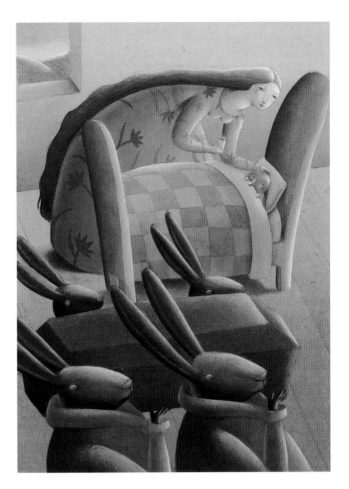

Books

1 (series)
Nicholas Wilton, illustrator
Andrea Cascardi, art director
John Grandits, designer
Mondo Publishing, client

Illustrations for the children's book *Right Outside My Window* by Mary Ann Hoberman. 16½ × 8½, acrylic on cement.

1

Books

1 (series)
Paul Kepple, illustrator/art director
Paul Kepple/Timothy Crawford, designers
Hotfoot Studio, layout
Headcase Design, design firm
Quirk Productions, Penguin Books, client

Series of two children's book diagrams from *The Witch's Handbook* by Rachel Dickinson.

2 Dick Krepel, illustrator
Jill Bossert, art director
Bernadette Evangelist, designer
Madison Square Press, design firm
Society of Illustrators, client

Cover of the *Society of Illustrators 43rd Annual of American Illustration*. 13 × 17, collage and digital.

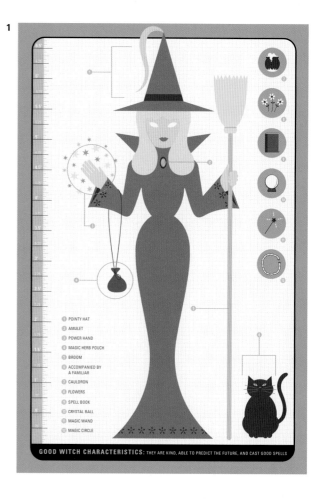

2

1

2

3

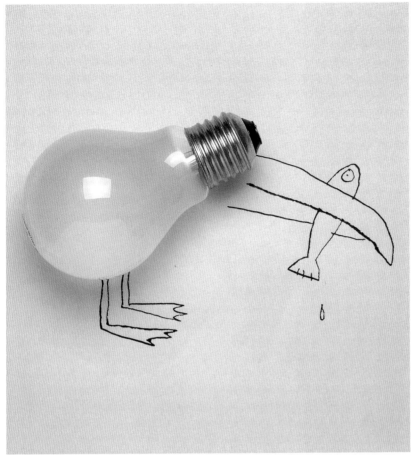

5

Books

1 Martin Jarrie, illustrator
Lynn Brofsky, art director
Lynn Brofsky Design, design firm
Beyond Words Publishing, client

Cover of *PowerHunch* by Marcia Emery, Ph.D.
8½ × 10, acrylic on paper.

2 Paul Davis, illustrator/art director/designer
Paul Davis Studio, design firm
University of California Press, client

Book jacket for John Lahr's *Show and Tell*.
Collage, acrylic and Photoshop.

3 Seymour Chwast, illustrator
Peter Buchanan-Smith, art director
The Ganzfeld, client

Illustration to accompany an article about Steven
Heller. 20 × 8½, pen line, colored digitally.

4 Serge Bloch, illustrator
Jürgen Kaffer, art director
Isabel Bünermann, designer
Buero Hamburg, design firm
Piper Publishing, client

Cover of *Das Beste aus dem Lexikon*
[Encyclopedia of Popular Errors]. Line art
photographed digitally with an object.

5 Stephen Chien, illustrator
Jonathan Howells, designer
Dinnick & Howells, design firm
Random House of Canada Limited, client

Book jacket of *The Final Confession of Mabel
Stark* by Robert Hough. 18 × 24, mixed media.

Books

1 Robert Crawford, illustrator
Nick Krenitsky, art director
Allson Donalty, designer
Harper Collins, design/client

Cover of Gloria Whelan's *Homeless Bird*, a book about a girl who rises out of poverty in India by making quilts. 16 × 20, acrylic on Masonite.

2 (series)
Lars Henkel, illustrator/art director
Anja Struck, design consulting
Reflektorium, design firm
Seb Cazes, Presse à Grumeaux, client

Series of illustrations from *Formalin Himmel*. 16 × 23, ink and Photoshop.

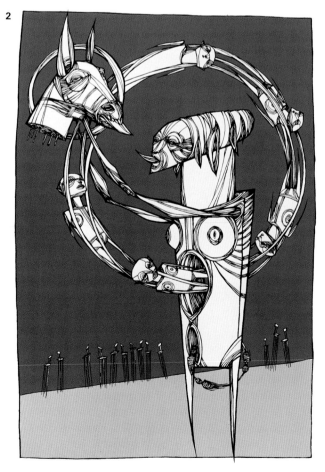

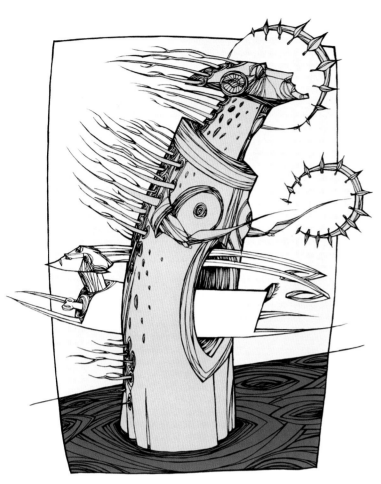
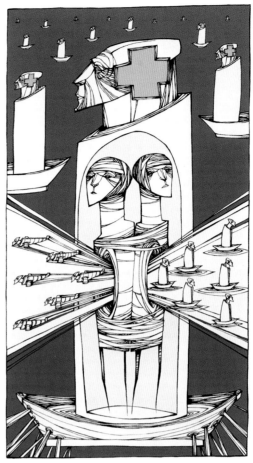
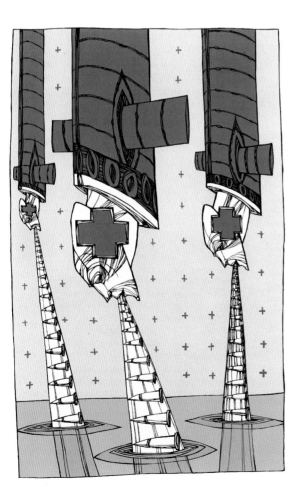
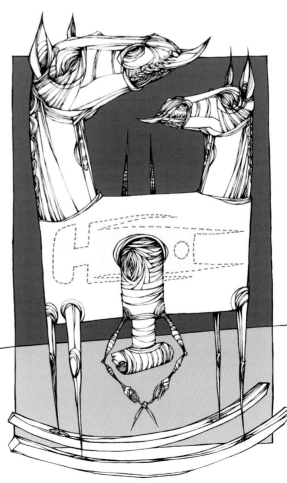

Books

1 Mark Summers, illustrator
Sonia Scanlin, art director
Yale University Press, client

   Cover of Joanne B. Freeman's *Affairs of Honor*. 12 × 9, engraving on scratchboard.

2 Marc Sutherland, illustrator
Howard Reeves, art director
Becky Terhune, designer
Harry N. Abrams, publisher/client

   Cover of *MacMurtrey's Wall* written and illustrated by Marc Sutherland. Mixed media.

3 Chris Gall, illustrator
Vikki Sheatsley, art director
Random House, client

   Cover of Julie Baker's *Up Molasses Mountain*, a book about a poor boy who wants to join the circus in Appalachia in the 1930s. 9 × 12, scratchboard and digital.

4 Paul Kepple/Timothy Crawford,
      illustrators/designers
Paul Kepple, art director
Headcase Design, design firm
Quirk Productions, Penguin Books, client

   Interior diagram of wizard characteristics for the children's book, *The Wizard's Handbook* by Caroline Tiger. 5³/₄ × 8³/₄, digital.

5 Alison Jay, illustrator
Jessica Dascher, designer
Chronicle Books, design/client

   Spread from *The Race*, a modern spin on an old fable.

1

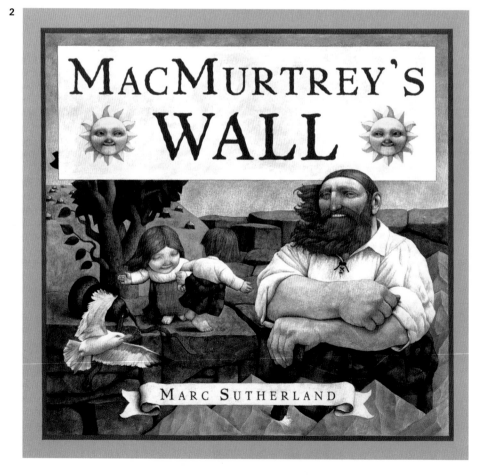

2

3

4

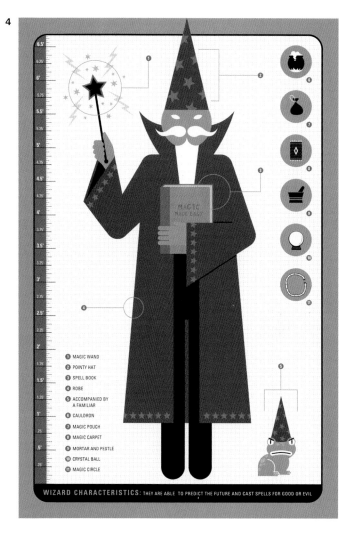

5

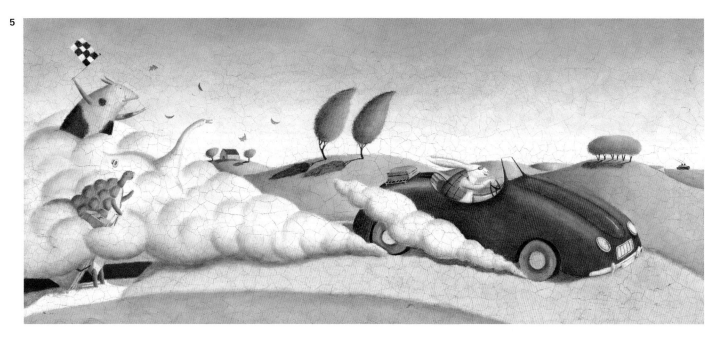

1

Books

1 (series)
Martin Matje, illustrator
Anne Diebel/Alexandra Balzer, art directors
Hyperion Disney, client

Illustrations from *A Pig Named Perrier* by
Elizabeth Spurr.

Books

1 (series)
Peter Kuper, illustrator
Monte Beauchamp, art director
Fantagraphics, client

Series of three from the *Blab* comic "Dreams of the Rarebit Fiend." Various sizes, mixed media.

2 Ashley Wood, illustrator
Ted Adams, art director
Robbie Robins, designer
IDW Publishing, client

Cover of *POPBOT*, a quarterly comic series by Ashley Wood. 8½ × 11, mixed media.

3 Henrik Drescher, illustrator/art director/designer
Arch MacDonald, Inhouse Design, typography
Chronicle Books, client

Cover of *Turbulence*, a log book by Henrik Drescher. 6½ × 8, mixed media.

4 Glin Dibley, illustrator/designer
Kate Gartner, art director
Knopf, client

Cover of Wendy Orr's book, *Nim's Island*, about a girl and her father on an island. 11 × 16, acrylic and pencil.

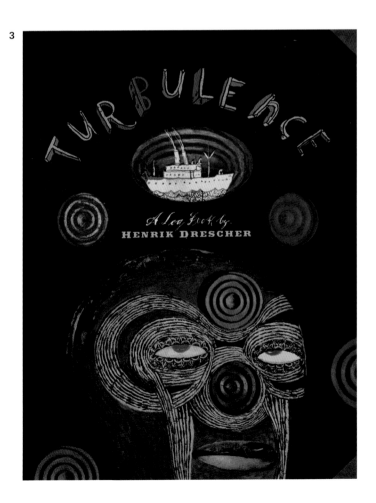

1

2

3

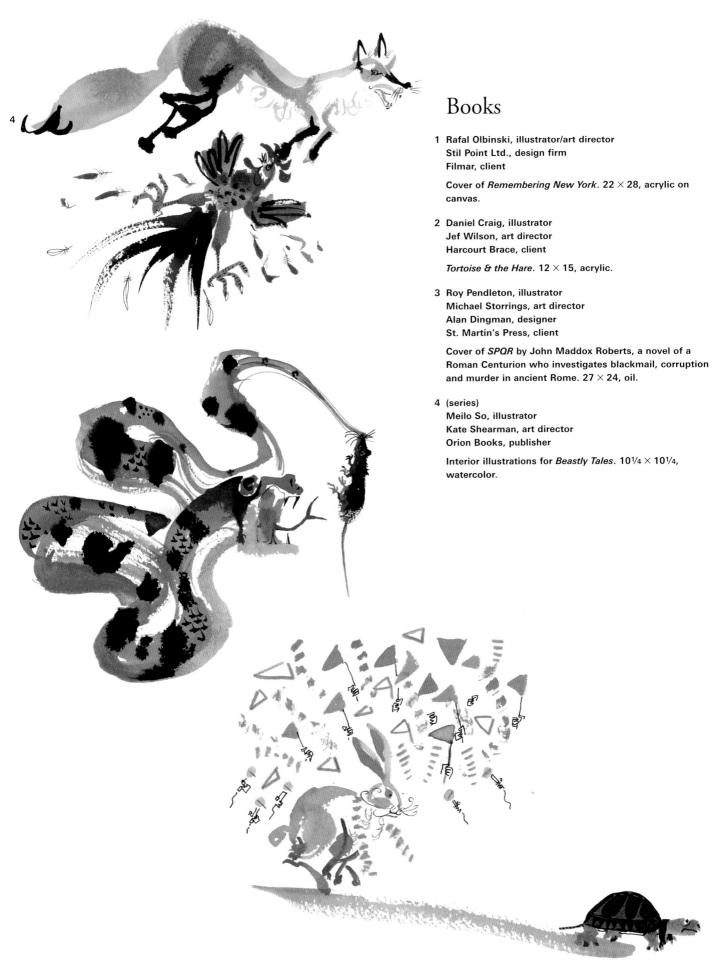

Books

1 **Rafal Olbinski**, illustrator/art director
Stil Point Ltd., design firm
Filmar, client

Cover of *Remembering New York*. 22 × 28, acrylic on canvas.

2 **Daniel Craig**, illustrator
Jef Wilson, art director
Harcourt Brace, client

Tortoise & the Hare. 12 × 15, acrylic.

3 **Roy Pendleton**, illustrator
Michael Storrings, art director
Alan Dingman, designer
St. Martin's Press, client

Cover of *SPQR* by John Maddox Roberts, a novel of a Roman Centurion who investigates blackmail, corruption and murder in ancient Rome. 27 × 24, oil.

4 (series)
Meilo So, illustrator
Kate Shearman, art director
Orion Books, publisher

Interior illustrations for *Beastly Tales*. 10¼ × 10¼, watercolor.

Books

1 Dennis Clouse/Traci Daberko, illustrators/designers
Francine Kass, art director
Cyclone Design, design firm
Simon & Schuster, client

Cover of Patricia Telesco's *How to be a Wicked Witch*.
5½ × 8½, mixed media.

2 Richard McGuire, illustrator
Sara Love, art director
Ali Karp, designer
Alink New Media, design firm
Graphic Artists Guild, client

Cover of the 10th edition of the *Graphic Artists Guild
Handbook: Pricing & Ethical Guidelines*.

3 Clemente Botelho, illustrator
Lisa Di Natale, art director
The Ghibeline Press, client

Cover of *Barber Shop Still Life: Tales of the City in the First
Person*, a book of short stories edited by Terence Watson.
Oil and acrylic on wood.

4 Andrea Ventura, illustrator
Italo Lupi, art director/designer
Abitare-Segesta, client

Portrait of Bertold Brecht from *Ritratti E Parole*, forty-one
portraits by Andrea Ventura. 13 × 18, mixed media.

1

2

3

Books

1 David Bowers, illustrator
Kathleen Flanigan, art director
Karin Paprocki, designer
Harper Collins, client

Cover of *A Tale of Time City* by Diana Wynne Jones,
a book about a girl taken into the future to save Time
City. 10½ × 17¼, oil on panel.

2 Glenn Harrington, illustrator
Chris Clarke/Roberta Knauf, art directors
McDougal Litter Publishing, client

Cover of junior high school literature textbook,
Don Quixote. 24 × 20, oil on linen.

3 Bill Cigliano, illustrator
Dawn Beard, art director
Harcourt Brace, client

Cover illustration for a fourth-grade reading book.
12 × 14, mixed media on board.

3

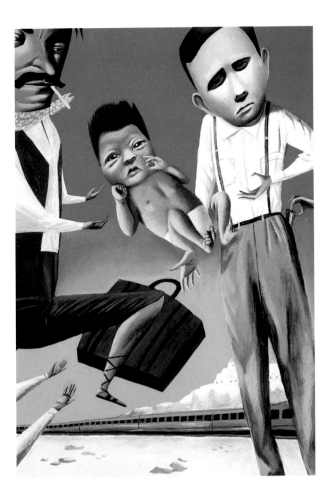

Books

1 (series)
Mark Ulriksen, illustrator
Frances J. Soo Ping Chow, designer
Running Press, publisher/client

Five illustrations from *The Complete and Totally True Book of Urban Legends* by Ann Fiery. Various sizes, acrylic on paper.

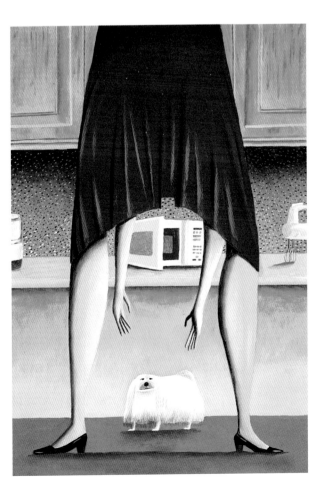

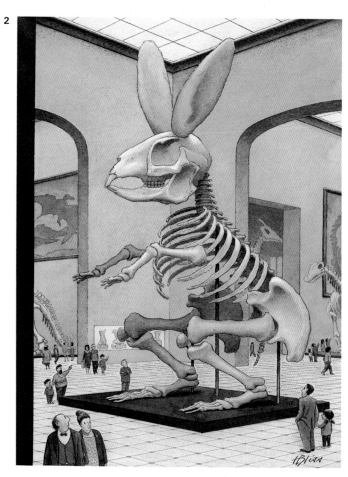

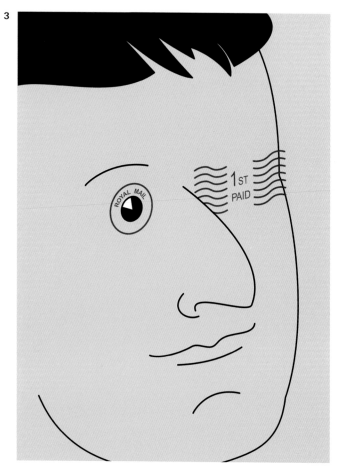

5

Editorial

1 Jason Holley, illustrator
   Hanna McCaughey, art director
   Marshall McKinny, designer
   Outside, client

   Article about looking for the possibly-extinct ivory-billed
   woodpecker. 12½ × 19⅜, mixed media.

2 Harry Bliss, illustrator
   Françoise Mouly, art director
   The New Yorker, client

   April 16, 2001 cover. 11 × 15, ink and watercolor.

3 Cyrus Deboo, illustrator
   Colin McHenry, art director
   Precision Marketing, design firm
   Centaur Communications, client

   Cover for a supplement about direct marketing.
   9½ × 13, digital.

4 Brian Cronin, illustrator
   Carol Macrini, art director
   Tamar Davis, designer
   Bloomberg Markets, client

   "Cross-Border Mergers Promises Unfulfilled." Big cross-
   border mergers are disappointing analysts and investors.
   6¾ × 9, goauche.

5 Jody Hewgill, illustrator
   Richard Baker, art director
   Christine Cucuzza, designer
   Premiere, client

   Portrait of Thora Birch for the video release of *Ghost
   World*. 9½ × 11½, acrylic on gessoed board.

6 Sarah Wilkins, illustrator
   Jane Palacek, art director
   Amy Shroads, designer
   Mother Jones, client

   Article, "Fighting Oil Drilling." Acrylic.

6

Editorial

1 Eddie Guy, illustrator
  Florian Bachleda, art director
  Vibe, client

  Portrait of Pastor Troy. 20 × 27, collage.

2 Ian Whadcock, illustrator
  Frank Tagariello, art director
  John Genzo, designer
  Bloomberg Personal Finance, client

  "Hothouse Treasures." Bonds sheltered from inflation's buffers
  have a place in any portfolio. Digital.

3 Chris Reed, illustrator
  Marge Dines, art director
  Kennel Quarterly, client

  Article exploring aggressive behavior, "Is it Learned or Inbred?"
  6 × 6½, digital color, pen and ink.

4 Jonathan Weiner, illustrator
  Patrick Prince, art director/designer
  Internet World, client

  "Selling the Psyche." How market shrinks use methods to
  measure Internet customers' behavior and needs. 16 × 24, oil.

5 Christopher Nielsen, illustrator
  John Yates, art director
  The Bulletin, client

  Article warning that retirees should only have offshore stocks as
  a small part of their portfolios, "Long Riders." 9 × 7½, acrylic.

3

4

5

Editorial

1 **David Hollenbach, illustrator**
Meg Birnbaum, art director
The American Prospect, client

Article on how Alabama judges use judicial overrides to disregard juries and impose death sentences, "The Judge as Lynch Mob."

2 **Jason Holley, illustrator**
Kevin Fisher, art director
Isabel De Sousa, associate art director
Audubon, client

The USDA wants to poison two million redwing blackbirds a year to save sunflower crops in the upper Midwest, "Red Baiting." 9 × 11, mixed media.

3 **Jody Hewgill, illustrator**
Robert Festino, assistant art director
Geraldine Hessler, design director
Entertainment Weekly, client

Portrait of Dave Matthews for an article about the unreleased "Lillywhite Sessions." These dark and brooding songs, which deal with death and mortality, have so far only been heard on Napster. 8 × 11, acrylic on gessoed board.

4 **Michael Sloan, illustrator**
Paul Virga, art director
Adweek, client

Cover for a special issue honoring the year's best creative ad campaigns. 8 × 10¼, gouache and digital.

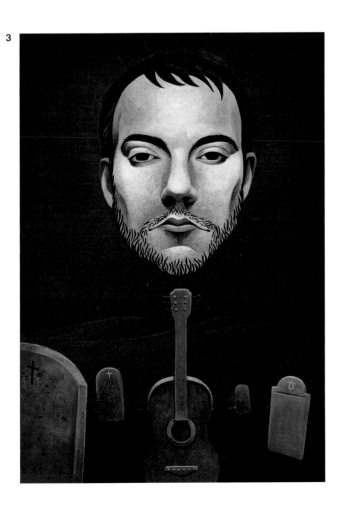

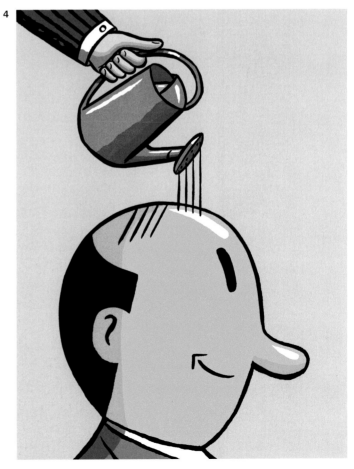

Editorial

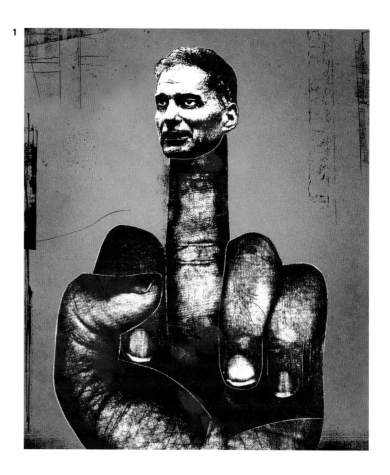

1 David Plunkert, illustrator
  Gail Anderson/Fred Woodward,
    art directors
  Gail Anderson, designer
  Rolling Stone, client

  "Ralph Nader is Not Sorry." 9 × 11,
  mixed media.

2 (series)
  Martin Jarrie, illustrator
  Frank Tagariello, art director
  John Genzo, designer
  Bloomberg Personal Finance, client

  An article about troubled markets making
  tax season more complicated for investors,
  "All the Right Tax Moves." Acrylic.

Editorial

3

1 PJ Loughran, illustrator
Tarver Harris, art director
Selling Power, client

Article about how to find the best locations for
business meetings. 10¾ × 10, digital.

2 Thomas Fuchs, illustrator
H.G. Pospischil, art director
Future, client

"The Great Innovators." 40 × 14, acrylic.

3 Gérard DuBois, illustrator
Laura Zavetz, art director
Beatrice McDonald, designer
Bloomberg Wealth Manager, design/client

"Escape Options." Underwater options have as
much ability to retain employees as the key to the
executive bathroom. How to find an escape route
from the trap of corporate stock options that may
lose their value. 9⅛ × 13¼, acrylic and collage.

4 Jonathan Carlson, illustrator
Melanie de Forest, art director
Fast Company, client

Article about a new amusement park. 7½ × 5,
brush/ink and digital.

Editorial

1 Joe Ciardiello, illustrator
  Kara Jones, art director
  Oxford American, client

  Ralph Stanley and Bob Dylan for the music issue. 7 × 8,
  pen and ink and watercolor.

2 Hadley Hooper, illustrator
  Jane Simon, art director
  Boston Globe Sunday Magazine, client

  Article about using new technologies to control and
  choose the information that you want while screening
  out what you don't, "Flood Control." 6 × 7, mixed media
  and digital.

3 Steven Guarnaccia, illustrator
  Cynthia Currie, art director
  Kiplinger's, client

  Back page, "The Lemons We Love." 11 × 13, pen and ink
  and watercolor.

4 Stephen Savage, illustrator
  Steven Heller, art director/designer
  New York Times Book Review, client

  Portrait of Andy Warhol. 3 × 3¼, digital.

5 Ruth Gwily, illustrator
  Amir Hadad, art director/designer
  Yedioth Achronot, client

  Newspaper article on pedophilia, "Keep out of the reach
  of children." 7¾ × 7¾, carbon paper and watercolor
  on paper.

1

2

The Lemons We Love

3

the main Squeeze

the Classic

the Stretch

the Velocipede

the Peel

5

Editorial

1 Gérard DuBois, illustrator
Jocelyne Fournel, art director/designer
L'Actualité, client

Opener for "Children of Divorce." 9⅞ × 13¼, acrylic.

2 Steve Moors, illustrator
John Klotnia, art director
Brad Simon, designer
Opto Design, design firm
Strategy & Business, client

Article about duality of China as it becomes one of the most powerful
financial countries while still maintaining its communist ideology.
8 × 10⅝, digital.

3 Art Spiegelman, illustrator
Françoise Mouly, art director
The New Yorker, client

November 26, 2001 cover. Digital.

4 James O'Brien, illustrator
Brian J. Noyes, art director
The Washington Post Magazine, client

Article about a gardener in Zambia who borrows money, "One Hand
Extended." The gardener taught the teacher what she needed to know
about Zambia, and her own delusions. 8 × 10½, digital.

1

Editorial

1 (series)
Calef Brown, illustrator
Frank Tagariello, art director
Bloomberg Personal Finance, client

Series of three images for "Here's looking at you."
The new new thing on the Net is account
aggregation—one-click access to your complete
financial picture.

2 Jason Holley, illustrator
Dirk Barnett, art director
Worth, client

Article about the migration of the power of the stock
market to Silicon Valley, "Wall Street Goes West."
14½ × 20 , mixed media.

3 C.F. Payne, illustrator
Jennifer Procopio, art director
Entertainment Weekly, client

Portrait of the cast of *Friends* at 75 years old. 13 × 16,
mixed media.

5

Editorial

1 **Istvan Banyai, illustrator**
   Françoise Mouly, art director
   The New Yorker, client

   September 10, 2001 cover. 8 × 11, pencil drawing and
   Photoshop.

2 **Gary Kelley, illustrator/art director**
   The North American Review, client

   Cover of the multicultural issue. 12 × 16, oil on canvas.

3 **Robert Neubecker, illustrator**
   Jon Houston, art director
   The New Republic, client

   Article on Chinese capitalism, "Trade Barrier." 8½ × 11,
   ink and digital.

4 **Hanoch Piven, illustrator**
   Janet Michaud, art director
   Time, client

   Bono, lead singer of U2, in the special global music issue.
   18 × 24, collage.

5 **David Hughes, illustrator**
   Geraldine Hessler, design director
   Entertainment Weekly, client

   Portrait of David Letterman. 24 × 24, mixed media.

6 **Lloyd Miller, illustrator**
   Minh Uong, art director
   Ted Keller, designer
   The Village Voice, client

   Feature on how genetically-modified food could be used
   to kill, "The DNA Bomb." 9⅝ × 12⅝, digital.

6

Editorial

1 Scott Laumann, illustrator
Ann Decker, art director
Fortune, client

Portrait of Alan Greenspan. 12 × 13, mixed media.

2 Nick Dewar, illustrator
Luke Hoyland, art director/designer
Mail & Guardian Media, client

Newspaper article on genetic testing during apartheid, "Project Coast—Apartheid Science." 6 × 8, acrylic.

3 Jeffery Decoster, illustrator
Karen Meyer, art director
The Taunton Press, Threads, client

Story about a woman who sews special clothes for her sister who has breast cancer, "Sewing Soothes Siblings' Souls." 13 × 15, acrylic on board.

4 Sterling Hundley, illustrator
Fred Woodward, art director/designer
Rolling Stone, client

Portrait of Kurt Cobain on the Table of Contents page commemorating the tenth anniversary of Nirvana's first album. 10 × 22, pen and ink and oil.

5 Nathan T. Ota, illustrator
Paul Gonzales, art director
Los Angeles Times, client

"You Can Say That and Worse." Shock radio, outrageous, lewd talk has become the norm. So who's going to stop it—the FCC? 9¾ × 6½, acrylic on board.

1

2

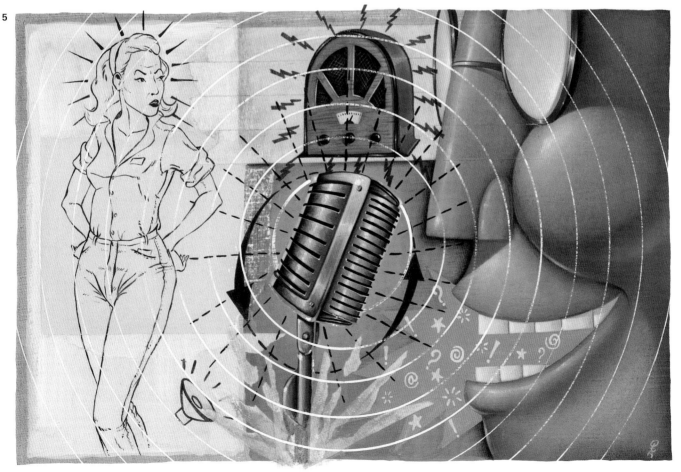

3

Editorial

1 Marc Rosenthal, illustrator
Tim J Luddy, deputy art director
Susan Scandrett, creative director
Business 2.0, client

"Great @ventures: A Digital Theme Park," the tech
and Internet industries are lampooned. 17 × 11½,
ink and watercolor.

2 Wesley Bedrosian, illustrator
Ann Decker, art director
Fortune, client

Article titled "Bad News Bearers Shift the Blame."
7½ × 5, watercolor and pen and ink.

3 Katherine Streeter, illustrator
Laura Zavetz, art director
Beatrice McDonald, designer
Bloomberg Wealth Manager, design/client

"Birds and Bees." When clients pass on, who will
advise the next generation? Take steps to ensure
that the advisor stays in the family. 11 × 11,
mixed-media collage.

4 Ward Schumaker, illustrator
Liz Hale, art director
Los Angeles Times Magazine, client

Portrait of the new aging Jimmy Carter.
9½ × 10½, Photoshop.

4

Editorial

1   Tim Zeltner, illustrator
    Jessica Reid, art director
    New Outlook, client

    Article about creating alternative income after retirement,
    "Securing your Future." 7 × 9, acrylic on wood.

2   Whitney Sherman, illustrator
    Steven Ramos, art director
    Forbes, client

    Article on managed health care: how laws, rules and insurance
    companies are making treatment of mental health problems
    confusing and less effective. 11 × 14, pencil and digital.

3   Joe Sorren, illustrator
    Kory Kennedy, art director
    Sports Illustrated, client

    Article about American pro tennis player Kimberly Po claiming
    to be Swiss in an international competition for fear of terrorist
    activity against Americans. 24 × 30, acrylic on canvas.

4   Christian Clayton, illustrator
    Janet Michaud, art director/designer
    Time, client

    Illustration from "Music Goes Global, Africa." 8 × 13, mixed
    media on paper.

4

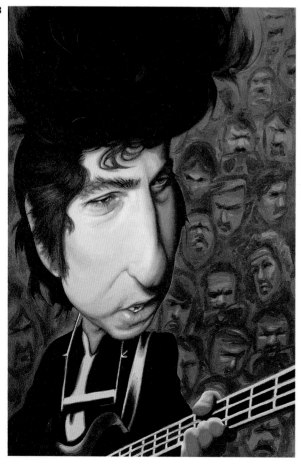

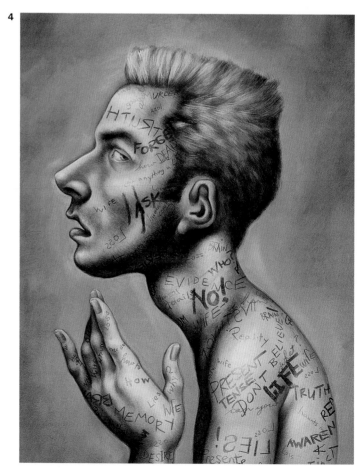

Editorial

1 **Jody Hewgill, illustrator**
   Gail Anderson, art director
   Andy Cowles, creative director
   Rolling Stone, client

   Portrait of Kasey Chambers, a country singer from Australia.
   9½ × 14, acrylic on gessoed board.

2 **Devon Bowman, illustrator**
   David Heath, art director
   Advisor's Edge, client

   Article about financial planners making choices, "Holding the
   future in their own hands." 5½ × 7¼, acrylic on paper.

3 **James Bennett, illustrator**
   Leonard Loria/Dave Nelson, art directors
   Yankee, client

   Article about Bob Dylan being booed at the Newport Jazz
   Festival in 1964, "Dylan Goes Electric." 12 × 17, oil on board.

4 **Anita Kunz, illustrator**
   Joe Kimberling, art director/designer
   Los Angeles Magazine, client

   Movie review of *Memento*. 11 × 14, mixed media.

5 **Craig Frazier, illustrator**
   Christine Silver, international art director
   Business Week International, client

   Article on the upcoming election in Italy, "Italy, Can
   Berlusconi Renew the Nation?" 8½ × 11, cut paper and
   digital.

6 **Balvis Rubess, illustrator**
   D.W. Pine, art director
   Arthur Hochstein, design director
   Time, client

   Article on phobias, illustrating the fear of chickens. 8 × 10½,
   acrylic and digital.

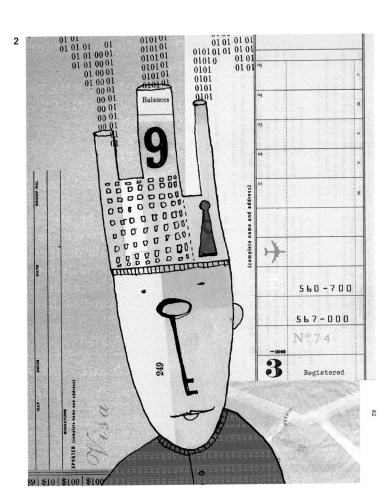

Editorial

1 **Phung Huynh, illustrator**
Cathy Gontarek, art director
The Pennsylvania Gazette, client

"Brain Power," science vs. religion and the use of alternate therapies. 8½ × 11.

2 **Jon Cannell, illustrator**
Kelly McMurray, art director/designer
Kelly Design, design firm
Computerworld, client

Article on self-serve applications on the Internet. 8⅝ × 11, pen and ink, collage and digital.

3 **Roger Chouinard, illustrator**
Wes Bausmith, art director
Los Angeles Times, client

"The Red Ink and Ken." How Ken Lay became rich at the expense of the company and the stockholders. 8 × 10, 3-D collage.

Editorial

1 Craig La Rotonda, illustrator
  Darlene Simidian, art director
  The American Lawyer, client

  Article about how law firms benefit from smart choices in office leasing, "Smart Leasing." 8 × 9, acrylic, collage.

2 Patrick Faricy, illustrator
  Minh Uong, art director
  Patrick Faricy/Minh Uong, designers
  The Village Voice, client

  Article on AIDS in Africa and the many parentless children left behind, "A Continent of Orphans—AIDS: The Agony of Africa." 8½ × 10¾, acrylic and colored pencil on illustration board.

3 Roberto Parada, illustrator
  Tom Staebler, art director
  Rob Wilson, designer
  Playboy, client

  "Bush vs. Clinton." 16 × 20, oil.

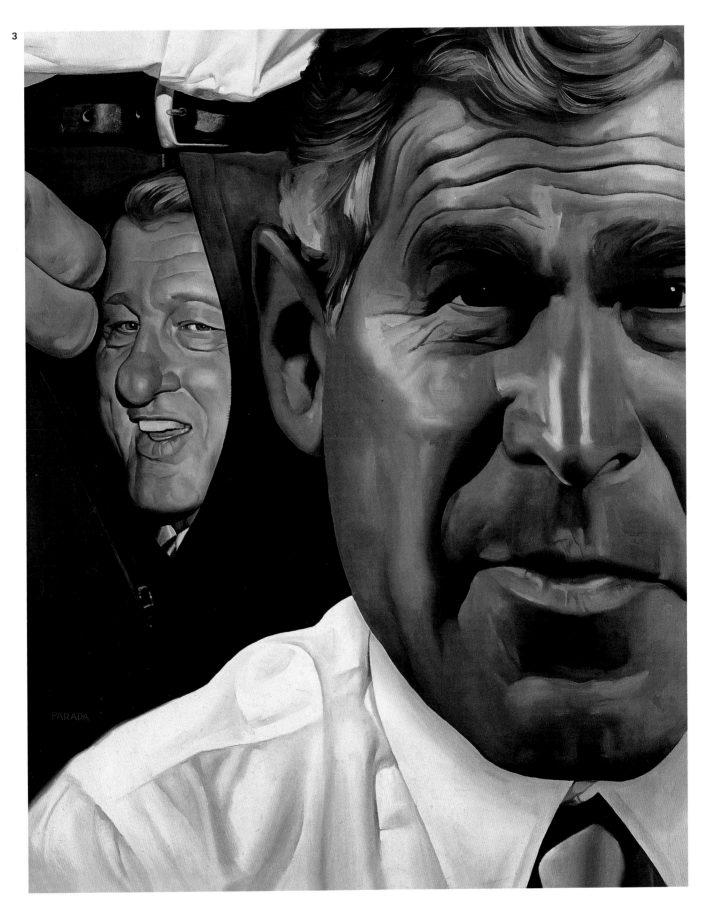

Editorial

1 Gene Greif, illustrator
   Alice Cheung, art director/designer
   Business Week, client

   Illustration for an article that asked investors, "Are you expecting too much?" 11 × 17, collage, acrylic and crayon.

2 (series)
   Anja Kroencke, illustrator
   Beatrice McDonald, art director
   Bloomberg Wealth Manager, client

   Article about the wealthy clientele of investment firms in Bel Air. Various sizes, mixed media and digital.

Editorial

1 Joe Sorren, illustrator
Laura Zavetz, art director
Bloomberg Wealth Manager, client

Article about divorce/family lawyers feeling as though they are stuck in the middle, like targets. 24 × 30, acrylic on canvas.

2 (series)
Anthony Freda, illustrator
Frank Tagariello, art director
Bloomberg Personal Finance, client

"Afterglow." Mixed media on wood.

Editorial

1 (series)
Conor Langton, illustrator
Simon Roche, art director
Hot Press, client

Images for new album reviews section: Missy Elliot, Bob Dylan, Björk,
Britney Spears and Alanis Morissette. Various sizes, acrylic.

The hill : hobbiton

Editorial

1 Jack Unruh, illustrator
   Lee Berresford, designer
   Geraldine Hessler, design director
   Entertainment Weekly, client

   "Elvish Lives!" The unlikely story of J.R.R.
   Tolkien, a tweedy Oxford professor whose
   beloved *Lord of the Rings* trilogy made him
   lord of the pop-culture realm. 13 × 13, ink
   and watercolor.

2 Linda Combi, illustrator
   Paul Webster, art director
   Charlie Haycock, designer
   Sainsbury's, The Magazine, design/client

   "A Word in Last" by Sue Townsend, humor-
   ously describes a weekend spent at an
   uncomfortable Elizabethan-themed hotel in
   England. Headline: I don't know if you've ever
   eaten an Elizabethan breakfast—a lump of grey,
   heavy-grained bread and butter curls from the
   fridge. 3¹/8 × 3¹/8, ink and collage.

3 Gahan Wilson, illustrator
   Tom Staebler, art director
   Kerig Pope, designer
   Playboy, client

   "The Invisible Man."

Editorial

1 John Kascht, illustrator
Geraldine Hessler, design director
Entertainment Weekly, client

Portrait of Michael Jackson, "Pop star from another planet: Will Michael Jackson's new album prove he's invincible?" 16 × 20, ink and watercolor.

2 Daniele Melani, illustrator
Vittorio Corona, art director/designer
Venti Quattro, client

"Matrimonio" for *Amica*. 11⁷/₈ × 14¹/₂.

3 Steven Dana, illustrator
Robert Dominguez, art director
Fortune, client

"You scratch my back, I'll scratch yours." Doing favors for each other in the business world. 3⁷/₈ × 5, mixed-media collage.

4 Geoffrey Grahn, illustrator
Gail Anderson, art director
Rolling Stone, client

Portrait of Shifty Shellshock, lead singer of Crazy Town, for the Table of Contents page. 5¹/₂ × 9¹/₄, scratchboard and digital.

5 Gérard DuBois, illustrator
Scolleen McCudden, art director
Selling Power, client

Article giving tips to CEOs, "Being in Control." 13⁵/₈ × 9³/₈, acrylic.

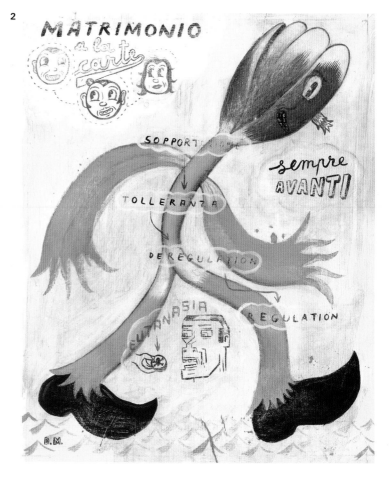

Editorial

1 Rick Meyerowitz/Maira Kalman, illustrators
Françoise Mouly, art director
The New Yorker, client

Cover of the December 10, 2001 issue. 11 × 17,
gouache on paper.

2 Mark Ryden, illustrator
Geraldine Hessler, design director
Entertainment Weekly, client

"Monkey D. We unearth tricks used in making the otherworldly
Planet of the Apes." 10 × 13, oil on panel.

3 Tim Hussey, illustrator
Patrick Prince, art director/designer
Internet World, client

"Personal Networks." 8 × 10, mixed media.

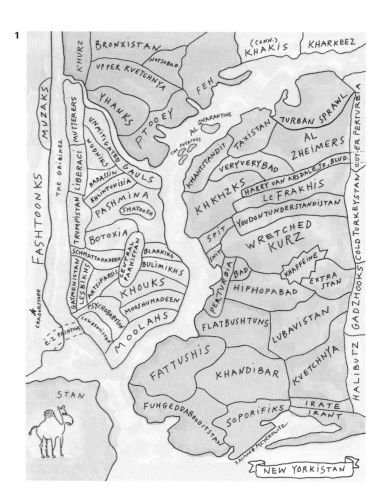

3

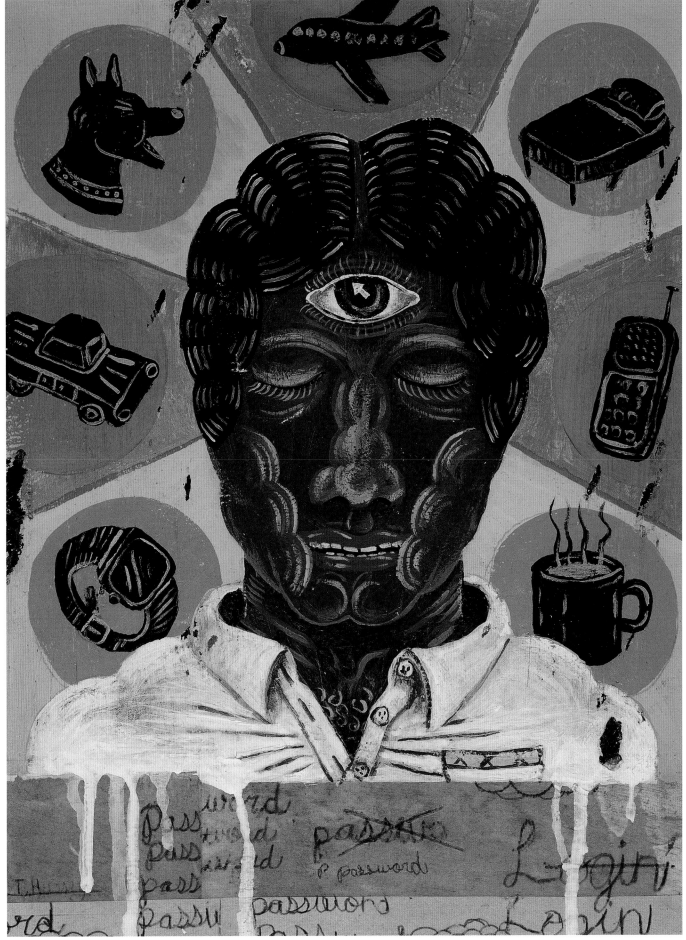

1

2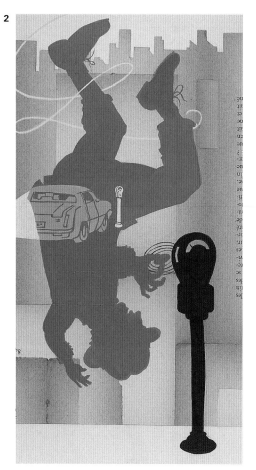

3

4

Editorial

1 Brian Rea, illustrator
   Leanne Shapton, art director
   Jason Logan, designer
   Saturday Night, The National Post, client

   "Left Behind" documents the difficulties and madness a Canadian politician faced along the campaign trail. 20 × 11, ball point pen.

2 Leigh Wells, illustrator
   Timothy Jones, art director
   Book Magazine, client

   Image accompanies a review of *Tepper Isn't Going Out* by Calvin Trillin. Mixed media.

3 Gary Baseman, illustrator
   Meilisa Lutner, art director
   Los Angeles Times, client

   Cover of the calendar section, "Yes, Virginia, there is a Halloween." Acrylic on canvas.

4 Greg Clarke, illustrator
   Tim J Luddy, deputy art director
   Susan Scandrett, creative director
   Business 2.0, client

   "The Decline (But Trust Us on This, Not the Fall) of the American Venture Capitalist." Despite their suffering many financial losses during the bursting of the dot-com bubble, most venture capitalists will continue to prosper. 6 × 8, watercolor on paper.

5 John Craig, illustrator
   Andrew Capitos, art director
   Red Herring, client

   "Every Million Counts." Article on a boss who bet his hair on cost cutting. Collage and digital.

5

Editorial

1 (series)
Paul Blow, illustrator
Frank Tagariello, art director
John Genzo, designer
Bloomberg Personal Finance, client

"Looking for Mr. Good Balance Sheet: These companies have lots of cash, low debt and real earnings."

2 Andrea Eberbach, illustrator
Dana Bussiere, art director
Digital Output Magazine, client

Cover. 8¹/₂ × 11, digital.

3 Yvetta Fedorova, illustrator
Bonnie Benwick, art director
Criss Stanford, designer
Washington Post, client

Article about a priest who does not want to compromise his beliefs and is taking a higher road, "If You Follow Me, Be Prepared to Take My Path." 3³/₄ × 5, collage.

4 Mick Wiggins, illustrator
Joe Yacinski, art director
Yacinski Design, design firm
Internal Auditor, client

"Hotel Fraud." Hotels as centers for a variety of fraud and embezzlement. 4¹/₂ × 11, digital.

5 Marc Rosenthal, illustrator
Tim J Luddy, deputy art director
Susan Scandrett, creative director
Business 2.0, client

"Doing More With Less." 8¹/₂ × 11¹/₄, ink and watercolor.

2

3

4

5

1

Editorial

1 Edel Rodriguez, illustrator
Owen Phillips, art director
The New Yorker, client

"Goings on About Town." Article on classic music conductor
Christophe von Dohnanyi. 8 × 8, pastel and woodblock,
ink on paper.

2 Catherine Lazure, illustrator
Frank Tagariello, art director
Diane Pavicic, designer
Bloomberg Personal Finance, client

Long-short funds play both the up- and downsides, "On the
Cutting Edge." Mixed media.

3 Claudia Pearson, illustrator
Gregory Smith/David Sebbah, art directors/designers
The New York Times Magazine, design/client

Fashion of the Times Part 2, Spring 2002. 14 × 17, acrylic.

3 1. "WHEN WE WINTERED IN *firenze*..." 2. "WHICH TRANSLATION DID YOU READ?" 3. "ANYTHING LOWER THAN A 410-THREAD COUNT, AND I CAN'T SLEEP." 4. "WHY BUY WASABI WHEN IT'S SO EASY TO MAKE?" 5. "IT'S JUST NEVER BEEN AN ISSUE; OUR KIDS WATCH MAYBE AN HOUR A WEEK." 6. "WE REALLY DO NEED ALL 10 PHONE LINES." 7. "YOU DON'T FLY COMMERCIAL, DO YOU?" 8. "YOU'RE KIDDING — YOU'RE STILL WORKING? WHOM DID YOU SAY YOU MARRIED?" 9. "A SIMPLE TREE ORNAMENT MEANS SO MUCH MORE TO US THAN AN EXPENSIVE PRESENT." 10. "PHIL AND I DECIDED WE HATE PARIS." 11. "THAT'S THE WAY THE KISSINGERS ARE. THAT'S WHY WE DON'T BOTHER WITH THEM ANYMORE." 12. "LAURA INSISTED WE STAY WITH THE FAMILY BECAUSE OF THE TAINT OF THE LINCOLN BEDROOM." 13. "THIS OLD THING? I DON'T KNOW. CHANEL OR SOMETHING." 14. "PEOPLE DO, BUT I WOULDN'T COOK ON ANYTHING BUT A VULCAN." 15. "WE DON'T EAT STILTON NOW THAT IT'S PASTEURIZED." 16. "NAN AND I STOPPED GOING TO THE GUGGENHEIM. IT'S TOO COMMERCIAL." 17. "WELTANSCHAUUNG? I DON'T THINK THERE IS AN ENGLISH EQUIVALENT." 18. "IT MUST HAVE BEEN ON CNN OR PBS, BECAUSE THOSE ARE THE ONLY STATIONS I WATCH." 19. "IS IT JEFFREY OR JERRY SEINFELD?" 20. "E-MAIL? IS THAT DIFFERENT FROM VOICE MAIL?" 21. "YOU KNOW WHERE SPIKE SITS? WE'RE BEHIND HIM, TO THE RIGHT OF BROKAW, ALMOST DIRECTLY OPPOSITE WOODY." 22. "IT'S SO HARD FOR ME TO GAIN WEIGHT. IT REALLY IS A PROBLEM." 23. "IF YOU HAVEN'T READ 'SUTRAS OF PATANJALI,' YOU SHOULDN'T EVEN BE TAKING YOGA CLASSES." 24. "WE DON'T CARE WHAT HE DOES AFTER COLLEGE. WE JUST WANT HIM TO BE HAPPY." 25. "WEREN'T YOU A FEW YEARS BEHIND ME IN NEW HAVEN?" 26. "WHEN MOTHER SHOT DR. TARNOWER —" 27. "YOU KNOW WHAT I HATE? *pretension.*" 28. "IT'S ONLY MONEY."

Editorial

1 (series)
Brad Yeo, illustrator
Guiv Rahbar, art director/designer
Yoga Journal, client

Article on the potential benefits, and what to consider when looking for guidance from a guru. 13 × 17, 10 × 12, acrylic.

2 Steve Brodner, illustrator
Chris Curry/Owen Phillips, art directors
The New Yorker, client

Portrait of Louis Freeh. 16 × 20, watercolor.

3 William Bramhall, illustrator
Lisa Zollinger Tobia, art director
Susan Syrnick, designer
Philadelphia Inquirer Sunday Magazine, client

Portrait of Ben Franklin for "Tough Town." 8³/₄ × 11, ink on paper.

4 Max Grafe, illustrator
Minh Uong, art director
The Village Voice, client

"Stalkers." 13¹/₂ × 10³/₄, mixed media on paper.

5 Jason Holley, illustrator
Susan Scandrett, creative director
Business 2.0, client

Article on a behavioral economist who explains the psychological principles which cause so many otherwise intelligent people to make dumb investment decisions, "Why Smart People Make Dumb Investments." 12 × 15, mixed media.

2

3

4

5

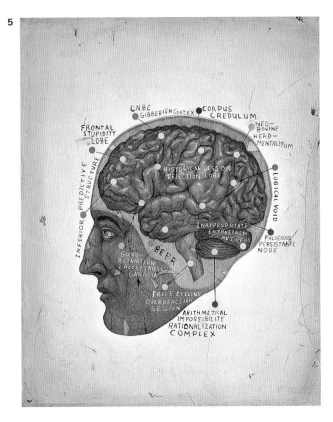

Editorial

1 **Rick Sealock**, illustrator
Shaun N. Bernadou, art director
Bike, client

Hoof and Mouth disease halts horseback riding in the United Kingdom, "Hoofn' What?" 9 × 12, mixed media.

2 **Dugald Stermer**, illustrator
Steven Heller, art director
The New York Times Book Review, client

Cover portrait of Dante Alighieri. 14 × 18, Derwent colored pencils.

3 **Marc Burckhardt**, illustrator
Lindsey Sipes, art director/designer
Oxford American, design/client

Portrait of bluesman Robert Johnson on the release of recordings from the 1920s and '30s. 11¹/₂ × 14, acrylic.

4 **Jason Holley**, illustrator
Tim J Luddy, deputy art director
Susan Scandrett, creative director
Business 2.0, client

Article about doing business in the recessionary economy, "Doing More with Less." 12 × 15, mixed media.

1

2

3

Editorial

1 Gérard DuBois, illustrator
Laura Zavetz, art director
Beatrice McDonald, designer
Bloomberg L.P., design
Bloomberg Wealth Manager, client

How to find an escape route from the
trap of corporate stock options that
may lose their value, "Escape
Options." 5 × 10, acrylic and collage.

2 Zach Trenholm, illustrator
Nancy Casey, art director/designer
The Portland Oregonian, client

Article on the career of Ringo Starr
and his upcoming concert.
6¹/₂ × 12¹/₂, digital.

3 Jason Holley, illustrator
Geraldine Hessler, art director
Tamaya Perry, designer
Entertainment Weekly, client

Spring movie preview. 11¹/₈ × 9,
mixed media.

4 Jordin Isip, illustrator
Stephanie Birdsong, art director
Fit Pregnancy, client

"Postpartum Depression." 8⁵/₈ × 12¹/₈,
mixed media on paper.

4

Isip

For Sale

1 (series)
Morgan Carver, illustrator
Arcadia Fine Arts, client

Gallery paintings: *Cowboys and Indians*; *Chinese Dragon*;
Destination, Moon; *Lost in Space* and *Lost Worlds*. 41 × 33;
22 × 17; 41 × 33; 30 × 24; 32 × 24, acrylic on panel.

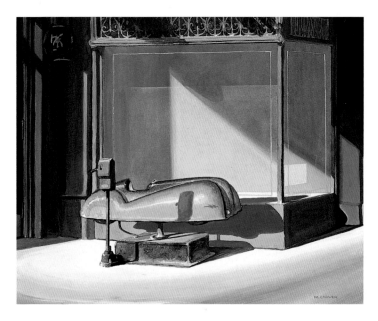

2

For Sale

1 David Scott Sinclair, illustrator
Sinc, art director
Burning Brush, client

Miracle of Science. 16 × 20½, acrylic.

2 (series)
Nicholas Wilton, illustrator/art director

Poppy, *Pear* and *Lily*. 8 × 8, acrylic on cement blocks.

1

For Sale

1 David M. Brinley, illustrator/art director/designer
Stigmatized for a gallery show. 18 × 24, acrylic on Masonite.

2 Shino Arihara, illustrator
For gallery sale. Gouache.

3 Timothy Cook, illustrator/art director/designer/design firm
Kensington-North Chevy Chase Ministerium, client
Image used to promote an interfaith worship service in response to September 11 and sold as prints to raise money for 9/11 victims. 5¹/₄ × 5³/₈, relief print.

Institutional

1 Melinda Beck, illustrator
Linda Meek, art director
Bruno Hohman, designer/design firm
J. Walter Thompson, ad agency
Ford Motor Company, client

Image for *Thunderbird Journal*. 6 × 7, pen and ink and digital.

2 Helen-Lenio Grohmann, illustrator/designer/design firm
Irene Tsolakis, art director
Amnesty International, client

Poster used to represent the Greek chapter of Amnesty International, *611*. 9¹/₂ × 11, acrylic.

3 Jason Holley, illustrator
Gary Williams, art director
Cahan & Associates, design firm
Maxygen, client

Annual report for a biotech company. 31¹/₄ × 22⁷/₈, mixed media.

4 Marco Ventura, illustrator
Bettina Ulrich, art director
Novum, client

Transgenic food. 8 × 11, oil on paper.

5 Steve Johnson/Lou Fancher, illustrators
Richard Spencer, art director
Susan Havice, designer
Great Source Educational Group, design/client

M is for Mask, one of a series of posters to encourage children to read. 11¹/₂ × 17¹/₂, oil on paper.

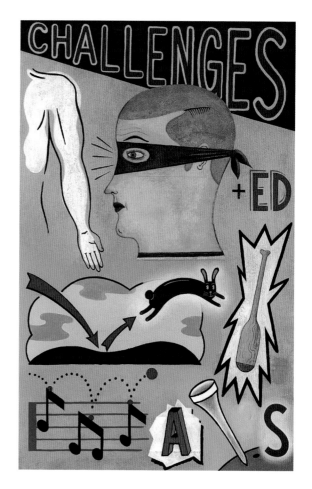

Institutional

1 (series)
Christian Northeast, illustrator
Su Mathews, art director/designer
Pentagram Design, design firm
Zurich Capital Markets, client

Rebus puzzle images created for a brochure: *When a Door Closes We Open a Window*, *Challenges are Masked Opportunities*, *Innovation is a Team Sport*, *You Can Not Drive Straight on a Twisting Road* and *What Strength Allows Agility Enables*. 9 × 15, mixed media.

2 Keith D. Skeen, illustrator
Mary Uttech, art director/designer
American Society for Quality, client

Taming your Web site. 18 × 16, acrylic.

Institutional

1 Isabelle Arsenault, illustrator
   Jeremy Linskill, art director
   Q-30 Design, design firm
   Osler, Hoskin & Harcourt LLP, client

   Cover of an outlook newsletter for an attorney's office.
   5¹/₂ × 6¹/₂, gouache.

2 Gregory Montfort Dearth, illustrator
   Tim Bade, art director
   Noble & Associates, ad agency
   Tyson Foods, client

   Poster for a sales program. 11 × 13¹/₂, scratchboard.

3 James Yang, illustrator
   Mindy Oswald, art director
   Brown University Alumni Magazine, client

   Illustration for "Reflections of a Student After 9/11."
   7 × 9, digital.

4 Philippe Lardy, illustrator
   David Armario, art director
   David Armario Design, design firm
   Deloitte & Touche, client

   Cover of annual report. 14 × 17, gouache.

5 Noah Woods, illustrator
   Carol Lasky, art director
   Cahoots, design firm
   Oxfam, client

   Poster for human rights organization. Mixed media.

6 Nicholas Wilton, illustrator
   Kimberly Baer, art director
   Kimberly Baer Design, design firm
   University of Judaism, client

   Poster depicting six aspects of Judaic life. 7¹/₄ × 11, acrylic
   on art board.

3

4

5
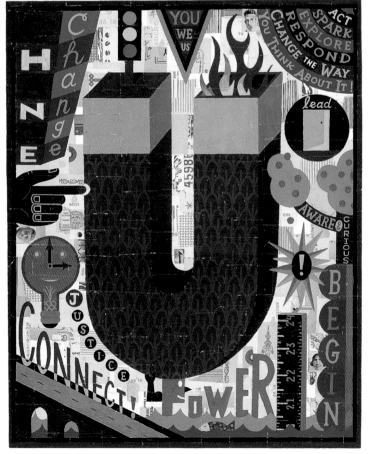

6

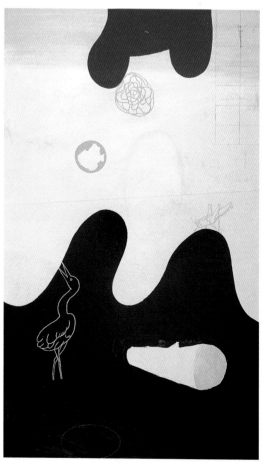

Institutional

1 (series)
  Jeffrey Decoster, illustrator/art director
  Jeffrey Decoster/Jenny Phillips, designers
  Jump Studio Design, design firm/client

  Design office panels that reflect the Japanese influences of
  the architecture. Each panel 30 × 40, acrylic, enamel and
  pencil on board.

2 Michael Bartalos, illustrator
  John Foster, art director/designer
  FUSZION|Collaborative, design firm
  U.S. Conference of Mayors, client

  Poster promoting the "City Livability Awards." 16 × 16, digital.

Institutional

1 **Chris Pyle, illustrator**
   Fred Fehlau, art director/designer
   The Phelps Group, design firm
   Playboy Jazz Festival, client

   "Jazz After Jazz" piece in the festival program. 8½ × 11, gouache on paper.

2 **Paul Wearing, illustrator**
   Mark Self, art director/designer
   Mark Self Design, design firm
   Consulting Psychologists Press, Inc., client

   Management training brochure. 11½ × 14⅞, digital.

Self-Promotion

Printed promotion for members of the graphic design industry such as illustrators, design firms, advertising agencies, printers, paper companies, art/design clubs and art schools.

3 **Mike Benny, illustrator**
   Bob Beyn, art director
   Seraphein Beyn, ad agency/client

   Leroy Robert Paige "Satchel" poster. 17 × 26, acrylic.

Self-Promotion

1 Gina Triplett, illustrator

   The Art of Camouflage, direct mail. 8½ × 7¾, acrylic and ink.

2 Dennis Clouse/Traci Daberko, illustrators/
      art directors/designers
   Cyclone Design, design firm/client

   Take Cyclone for a Spin poster. 17 × 8½, mixed media.

3 (series)
   Riccardo Stampatori, illustrator
   Steffanie Lorig/Riccardo Stampatori, art directors
   Steffanie Lorig, designer
   American Institute of Graphic Arts, client

   Door knob signs for the Art with Heart program for hospitalized children. 10 × 20, acrylic on wood.

Self-Promotion

1 Jordin Isip, illustrator

Floating, a postcard. 3½ × 5½, ink and acrylic on paper.

2 Tim Bower, illustrator
Joe Ciardiello, art director
Patrick J.B. Flynn, designer
PJBF Design, design firm
Society of Illustrators, client

Print ad for the Call for Entries 44. 16 × 20, gouache.

3 Nicholas Wilton, illustrator
Scott Ray, art director
Peterson & Co., design firm
Dallas Society of Visual Communications, client

Cover image of *Rough*. 10 × 16, acrylic on wood.

4 (series)
Renata Liwska, illustrator
Steve Pearson/Robert Sweetman, art directors
Bryan Collins, writer
Brown Communications, ad agency
Ad Rodeo Award Show, client

Tarot cards for advertising award show: *The Brief*, *The Budget*, *Execution* and *The Podium*. Mixed media and digital.

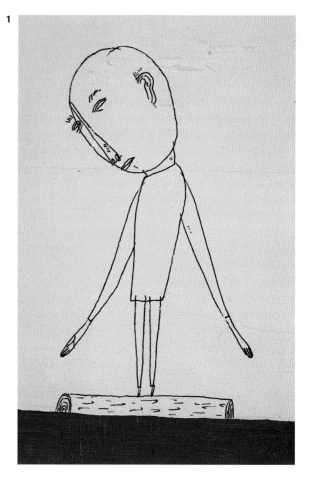

4

Self-Promotion

1 Brad Holland, illustrator/art director/designer
  The Illustrators' Partnership of America, client

  Cover of *The Future of Illustration* video box. 3¹/₂ × 6³/₈, ink.

2 (series)
  Luba Lukova, illustrator/designer
  Luba Lukova Studio, design firm
  The Alternative Pick, client

  Creative resource directory for the advertising and editorial industries. 8¹/₂ × 8¹/₂, tempera.

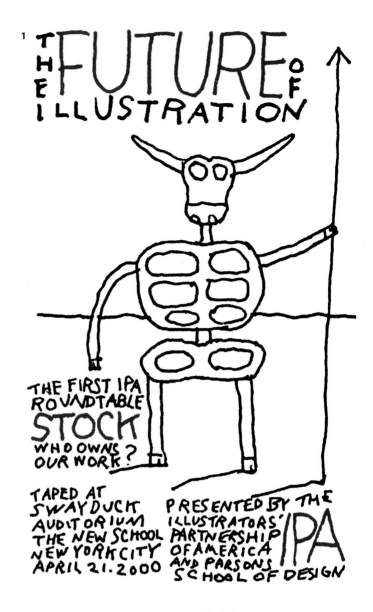

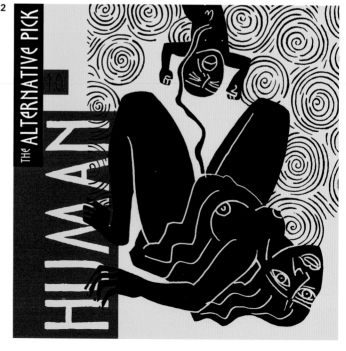

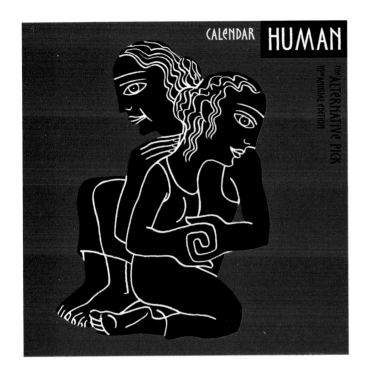

1

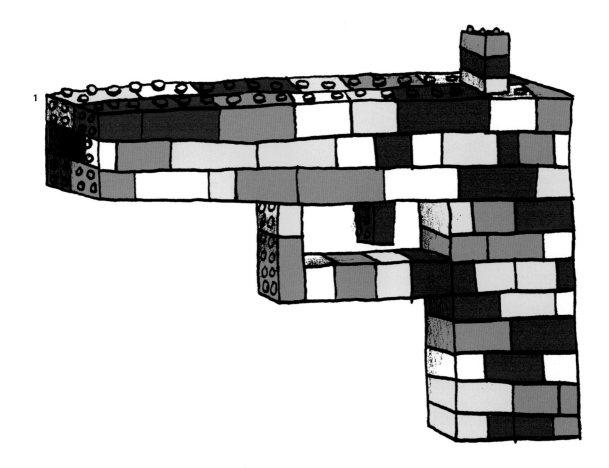

2

Self-Promotion

1 Julian Trout, illustrator/client

Lego Handgun for promotional print and Web site. 10 × 9, ink and digital.

2 Joe Sorren, illustrator
The Alternative Pick, client

Upon Teresa at the Dot, used in a source book ad. 60 × 48, acrylic on canvas.

3 (series)
Daniel Baxter, illustrator/client

Images used in a source book of illustration. Originally created to promote the *New York Times* Travel and Sports sections, art director/designer Sharon Driscoll. Each 8³/₄ × 5⁵/₈, pen and ink, collage and digital.

4 Susan Todd, illustrator

Tattooed Lady, mailer. Linocut and digital.

Self-Promotion

1 Joe Sorren, illustrator
Renee Rech, art director/designer
Renee Rech Design Inc., design firm
YUPO Papers, client

Ela elppa's apple ale, palindrome for 2002
calendar. 24 × 24, acrylic on canvas.

2 Linda Helton, illustrator
Laurie Riggin/Patricia Kowalczyk,
 art directors
Olver Dunlop Associates, design firm
Marlena Agency/Olver Dunlop
 Associates, clients

Calendar image based on a quote by the Dalai
Lama. 11 × 11, acrylic.

3 Juliette Borda, illustrator
Mark Murphy, art director/designer
Murphy Design, design firm

Outer Space calendar image. 7¹/₂ × 7¹/₂,
gouache on paper.

2

Self-Promotion

1 Michael Kerbow, illustrator/art director/designer
Skeleton, design firm/client

Promotional mailer for a digital art studio. Digital.

2 John Ueland, illustrator

School Violence, used for a direct-mail promotion sent to editorial clients. 6 × 6³/₄, digital.

3 Joe Sorren/Eric White, illustrators
La Luz de Jesus, client

Ad for a gallery show, *That Which Organizes My Feathers*. 36 × 30, acrylic on canvas.

3

Self-Promotion

1 (series)
Nicholas Wilton, illustrator/art director
Mark Murphy, designer
Murphy Design, design firm

Series portraying aliens. 8 × 8, acrylic on cement blocks.

2 Nathan Jurevicius, illustrator/design
Desktop, client

Promoting www.nathanj.com.au for the magazine's special on Australian illustrators. Digital.

3 Amy Crehore, illustrator

Homage to the King of Cats, postcard mailer. 18 × 22, oil on linen.

4 Traci Daberko/Dennis Clouse, illustrators/
art directors/designers
Cyclone Design, design firm/client

Poster, *The Cyclonic*. 17 × 8½, mixed media.

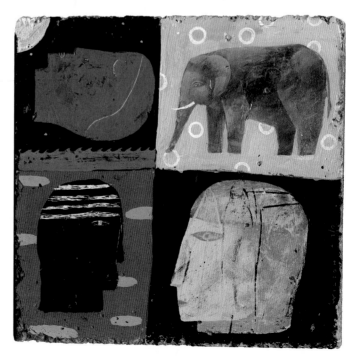

2

3

4

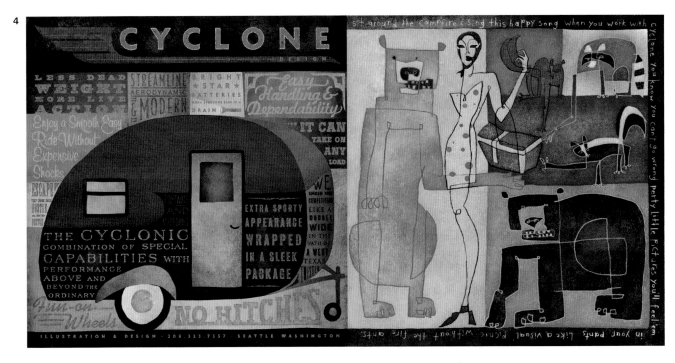

Self-Promotion

1 Jacob Escobedo, illustrator

Mailer, portrait of Gene Hackman as "Royal" from the film *The Royal Tenenbaums*. 17 × 22, mixed media.

2 Colin Johnson, illustrator

Boxing promotional card. 8¹/₂ × 11, mixed media.

Unpublished

3 Loren Long, illustrator
Martha Rago, art director
David Caplan, designer

Interior piece from the soon-to-be-released children's book, *The Wonders of Donal O'Donnell* by Gary Schmidt. 26 × 12, acrylic.

© 2002 Loren Long

4 Isabelle Arsenault, illustrator

Two Different Points of View: Similarities and Differences Between People. 8 × 7¹/₄, gouache.

© 2002 Isabelle Arsenault

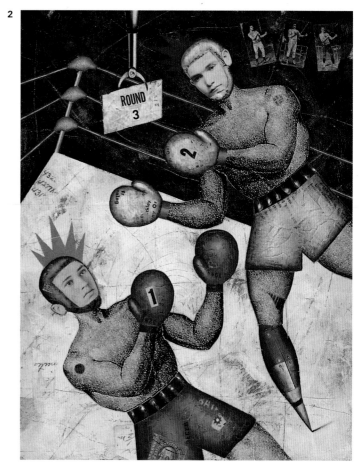

3

4

1

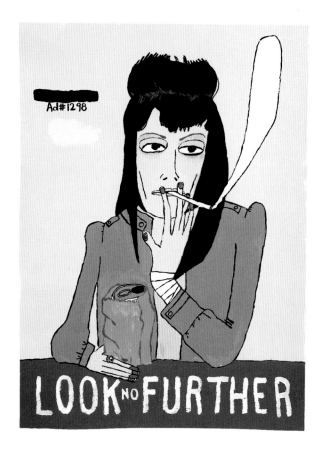

2

Unpublished

1 (series)
Esther Pearl Watson, illustrator

Illustrations are inspired by personal ads.
16 × 20, acrylic.

© 2002 Esther Pearl Watson

2 Braldt Bralds, illustrator
Margaret Nelson, art director
Bralds Nelson Design, design firm

Cover for *Purrsonalities Profiles*, an unpublished
book project. 10 × 10, oil on panel.

© 2002 Braldt Bralds

3 Clayton Brothers, illustrators/
    art directors/designers

Portfolio piece. Mixed media on canvas.

© 2002 Clayton Brothers

3

1

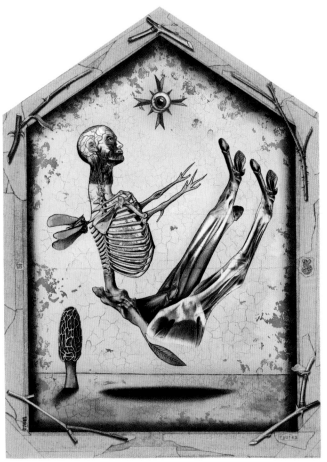

Unpublished

1 (series)
Pol Turgeon, illustrator/art director

Series from *Corpus Herbarius*: *Skull*; *Post Vitam Somnium*;
Falling Figure; *Butterfly*; and *Apertura*. 13½ × 18, mixed media.

© 2002 Pol Turgeon

2 Keith Dixon, illustrator/art director/designer
N8 Design, design firm

Unpublished book project, *The Cup is Half Full*, showing the
positive aspects of being alone. 8 × 12, digital, mixed media.

© 2002 Keith Dixon

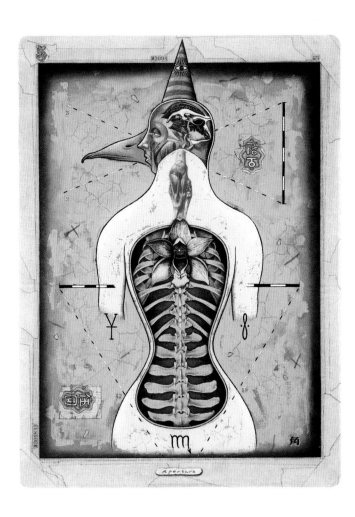

Unpublished

1 Daniel Bejar, illustrator

Personal piece, *Cement Shoes*. 11 × 14, monoprint.

© 2002 Daniel Bejar

2 Marie-Andrée Bureau, illustrator

Personal project: *Barking up the wrong tree*. Exploration of contrasting and complementary imagery.

© 2002 Marie-Andrée Bureau

3 (series)

Poul Hans Lange, illustrator

Aesop's Fables. Various sizes, collage and mixed media.

© 2002 Poul Hans Lange

3

THE CAMEL.

WHEN man first saw the Camel, he was so frightened at his vast size that he fled away. After a time, perceiving the meekness and gentleness of his temper, he summoned courage enough to approach him. Soon afterwards, observing that he was an animal altogether deficient in spirit, he assumed such boldness as to put a bridle in his mouth, and set a child to drive him.

Use serves to overcome dread.

THE FABLES OF ÆSOP.

RETURNED TO SENDER

THE TWO BAGS.

EVERY man, according to an ancient legend, is born into the world with two bags suspended from his neck—a small bag in front full of his neighbors' faults, and a large bag behind filled with his own faults. Hence it is that men are quick to see the faults of others, and yet are often blind to their own failings.

A Fox entered the house of an actor, and, rummaging through all his properties, came upon a Mask, an admirable imitation of a human head. He placed his paws on it, and said, "What a beautiful head! yet it is of no value, as it entirely wants brains."

THE FOX AND THE MASK.

THE CRAB AND ITS MOTHER.

A CRAB said to her son, "Why do you walk so one-sided, my child? It is far more becoming to go straightforward." The young Crab replied: "Quite true, dear mother; and if you will show me the straight way, I will promise to walk in it." The mother tried in vain, and submitted without remonstrance to the reproof of her child.

Example is more powerful than precept.

THE FOX AND THE GRAPES.

A FAMISHED FOX saw some clusters of ripe black grapes hanging from a trellised vine. She resorted to all her tricks to get at them, but wearied herself in vain, for she could not reach them. At last she turned away beguiling herself of her disappointment and saying: "The Grapes are sour, and not ripe as I thought."

Unpublished

1 (series)
Cindy Eunyoung Kim, illustrator

Images of East Los Angeles. Various sizes, acrylic, pen and ink on collaged paper.

© 2002 Cindy Eunyoung Kim

Unpublished

1 Keith Dixon, illustrator/art director/designer
N8 Design, design firm

Unpublished book project; *The Cup is Half Full*, showing the positive aspects of saying good-bye. 8 × 12, digital, mixed media.

© 2002 Keith Dixon

2 Anita Kunz, illustrator/art director

Image about cloning. 12 × 12, mixed media.

© 2002 Anita Kunz

3 (series)
Will Bullas, illustrator

The Storkbroker; *Blind Pig and Mummy Dog*; *The Elephant in the Corner*; *The Booze Hound*; and *The Cattle Hustler*. Various sizes, watercolor.

© 2002 Will Bullas

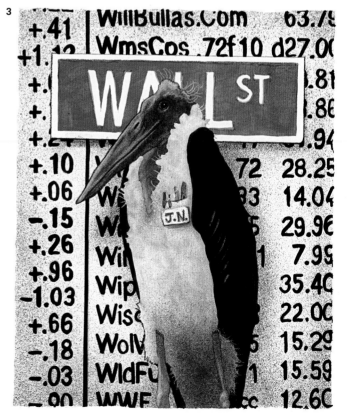

Unpublished

1 Anna Tillett, illustrator

The Twelve Dancing Princesses With Two Left Feet. 8 × 10, acrylic on canvas, digital.

© 2002 Anna Tillett

2 Joe Sorren, illustrator
Charlie Kropp/Marie Kropp, clients

My piano teacher as a young girl, *Portrait of Marie*. 24 × 30, acrylic on canvas.

© 2002 Joe Sorren

3 (series)
Stefano Vitale, illustrator
Jo Ann Hill, art director
Melissa Nelson, designer

Series for an upcoming book to be published by Clarion. *Can You Guess My Name, Traditional Fairy Tales From Around the World*: Burma, USA, Japan, Italy and Sweden. 10 × 12, oil, acrylic and gouache.

© 2002 Stefano Vitale

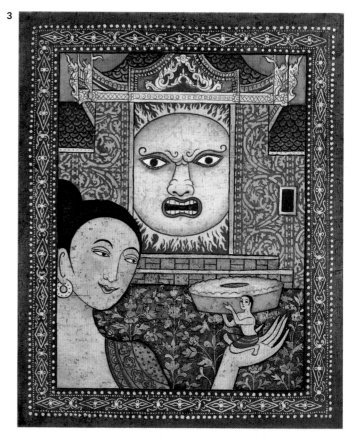

Unpublished

1 Keith Dixon, illustrator/art director/designer
   N8 Design, design firm

   Unpublished book project; *The Cup is Half Full*, showing the negative
   aspects of saying good-bye. 8 × 12, digital, mixed media.

   © 2002 Keith Dixon

2 (series)
   Paul Davis, illustrator/art director/designer
   Paul Davis Studio, design firm

   Images for an exhibition: *Uncle Bunny*; *Dusty*; *Myrna*; *The Real Me*;
   and *Lenore*. All 12 × 16, acrylic on canvas, except *Dusty* (on paper),
   9¹/₄ × 12³/₈,

   © 2002 Paul Davis

Unpublished

1 Jason Holley, illustrator
Bruce Ramsey, art director

Unpublished *Newsweek* cover showing the changing
face of Christianity. 23¹/₅ × 30⁵/₈, mixed media.

© 2002 Jason Holley

2 Leigh Wells, illustrator

Personal piece: *Where I Sit*. Mixed media.

© 2002 Leigh Wells

Cougar. Looks Good in Metallics.

COUGAR OPAQUE IS PERFECT FOR ATTENTION-GRABBING TECHNIQUES LIKE METALLIC INKS AND FOIL-STAMPING, AND ITS SMOOTH SURFACE KEEPS DOT-GAIN TO A MINIMUM, SO YOUR IMAGES STAY CRISP AND SHARP. WHEN YOU WANT TO MAKE A BIG IMPACT BUT YOU DON'T HAVE A BIG BUDGET TO MATCH, USE COUGAR. NO OTHER PAPER DELIVERS SO MUCH FOR SUCH A REASONABLE COST. TO FIND OUT MORE VISIT WWW.COUGAROPAQUE.COM.

Weyerhaeuser
The future is growing™

Printed on 100 lb. Cougar® Opaque, Smooth Finish.
Printed on a UV Press utilizing Interdeck UV drying using a size
varnish, Williamson's Liquid Foil℠ and 4 color process.

Editor's Column

BY PATRICK COYNE

Considering the difficult economic climate, we were quite surprised to see a 9.8% jump in entries to this year's *Illustration Annual*, making it our biggest ever. A closer inspection of the 7,207 entries revealed that most of the growth was in the self-promotion and unpublished categories. The high point of this year's competition though was books, which had its strongest showing in years.

Looking over the winners, you'll see solutions ranging from the primitive to the tightly rendered—that speaks of the incredible diversity in the field today. And, despite receiving over half our reproduction materials as digital files, acrylic is surprisingly still the medium of choice, followed closely by mixed media.

This year's jurying began on Sunday morning, April 7th. We worked in two large conference halls, each equipped with a projector for slide entries and six rows of tables for tear sheets and proofs.

The jurors worked in two groups of three with Jean Coyne acting as the sixth judge during the screening. All but the smallest categories had been divided so each team screened half of the entries submitted. The judges alternated between viewing a carousel of slides and then a set-up of print entries. Any juror could place an illustration in the finals by handing a printed piece to a member of the CA crew. Slide entries were screened by checking the "in" or "out" column on prepared scoring sheets.

The final voting took place on Monday with all five jurors working together. Print entries were again spread out on the tables. Two paper cups, one white for "in," the other red for "out," with slots cut in the bottom, were placed upside down to the right of the pieces. The jurors voted by putting a different colored tile into the bottom of the appropriate cup. The different colored tiles allowed us to make sure that every entry was voted on by every judge. Finalists submitted on slides were again voted on by each juror checking "in" or "out" on scoring sheets.

A minimum of four votes was required for acceptance and all entries were treated as equals in the design of the Annual.

I would like to thank all of the judges for their conscientious efforts in selecting our 43rd *Illustration Annual*.

Kristi Anderson is currently in her second stint as art director of *Utne Reader*—a magazine of alternative ideas and culture—based in Minneapolis, Minnesota. She was AD there for four years in the early 1990s, then left for motherhood and the freelance life. She's been back with *Utne* now for three years, juggling the job with her work as art director of *Riverbank Review of Books for Young Readers*, and at Two Spruce Design, a small firm she continues to run with her husband, designer and artist Scott Anderson. Prior to joining *Utne Reader*, she was an associate art director at Whittle Communications in Knoxville, Tennessee. She combined studies in graphic design and journalism to earn a B.A. from Iowa State University in 1985. Her work has been recognized in *Communication Arts* and *Print* magazines.

Braldt Bralds first learned of the profession of illustration from magazine advertisements while a small child in The Netherlands. When he was twelve he began attending the Grafische School in Rotterdam, where he was instructed in graphic arts and learned the intricacies of the printing

Photography by K. Gypsy Zaboroskie

Editor's Column

trade. Since moving to the United States in 1979, his work has appeared in *Time, Newsweek, Der Spiegel, Omni, Rolling Stone, Atlantic Monthly* and *National Geographic*. In addition, he has illustrated book covers, advertising campaigns and designed postage stamp sets for the United Nations as well as the United States Postal Service. Braldt, who received the Hamilton King Award from the Society of Illustrators in 1984, lives in Santa Fe, New Mexico.

Gaby Brink is co-founder and creative director of Templin Brink Design in San Francisco. After graduation from California College of Arts and Crafts, she began her career at Pentagram Design and Vanderbyl Design in San Francisco. In 1995, she joined Foote, Cone & Belding as one of the first members of their internal design group, initially created to address Levi Strauss & Co.'s retail design needs. Gaby left FCB in 1998 to found Templin Brink Design along with her business partner Joel Templin. Her work has been recognized by virtually every international design award including *Communication Arts, Graphis*, the New York Art Directors Club, The One Show, the American Institute of Graphic Arts, the New York Type Directors Club, *ID* magazine and *Print*'s Design Annual.

Donna Mark has been a senior designer at Henry Holt Books for Young Readers in New York City since 1999. She began her career over eleven years ago in the art department for Putnam and Philomel Books, both divisions of Penguin Putnam. Donna's design efforts have been seen on a Randolph Caldecott Medal-winning book as well as a National Book Award, Young People's Literature winner. Mark holds a degree in Visual Arts from Rutgers University where she initially intended to major in engineering. An avid balletomane, Donna divides her time between Manhattan and the shore points of New Jersey.

Frank Tagariello is the art director of *Bloomberg Personal Finance* magazine based in Princeton, New Jersey. Born in New York City, Frank received a Bachelor of Fine Arts from Pratt Institute. He has worked for such publications as *Travel & Leisure, Geo, The New York Times Sunday Magazine, Harper's Bazaar, Redbook* and *Smart Money*. Since helping to launch *Bloomberg Personal Finance* five years ago, the magazine has been the recipient of numerous art awards and nominations, including the American Society of Magazine Editors (design and photography), *Communication Arts*, American Illustration, American Photography annuals and the Society of Publication Designers. Frank, who is an avid photographer, currently resides in South Bound Brook, New Jersey, with his two teenage sons and is currently in the process of renovating his 200-year-old house. ■

Braldt Bralds

Donna Mark

Kristi Anderson

Gaby Brink

Frank Tagariello

Six Degrees™

timefreeing technology™

Get absolutely organized.
Change absolutely nothing.

Now you can be perfectly organized without having to change
the way you work. Every email message and document in your
computer will always be right at your fingertips, regardless of
where you file it – or misfile it.

Six Degrees™ software from Creo lets you navigate through
projects in a powerful new way by uncovering connections
between messages, files and people – right on your desktop.
It helps you spend less time organizing your work and more
time doing it.

Be as disorderly as you like and let Six Degrees keep you from
being disorganized – absolutely – without changing a thing.

Download Six Degrees FREE for 30 days:

getsixdegrees.com

Adobe

Multiple undos. Because bad things happen in threes.

Or fours, or fives. But, luckily, it doesn't matter. Because with our unlimited
number of undos and redos you'll be able to return your file to the happy place it once was.
To learn more, take a test drive at www.adobeindesign.com.

Adobe® InDesign® 2.0 | Tools for the New Work.

Contributors

Columns

Roger Whitehouse was trained as an architect in England before coming to the United States in 1967 to teach design at Columbia University. His multidisciplinary design studio, Whitehouse & Company, founded in 1976, has completed projects as far ranging as graphics for the High Museum in Atlanta, Lincoln Center and The Metropolitan Museum of Art in New York, and most recently, signage for the Condé Nast and Reuters buildings and the Flagship Subway entrance on 42nd Street, all in Times Square. He is probably best known for his universal design work for differently-abled individuals. He has been a vice president of AIGA and a director of SEGD. Roger wrote the Design Issues column, edited by DK Holland.

John Paul Caponigro, author of *Adobe Photoshop Master Class*, is an internationally-respected fine artist whose work resides in numerous collections including Estée Lauder and the Smithsonian. His clients include Canon, Epson, Apple, Adobe, Imacon and Kodak. He is a contributing editor to *View Camera* and *Camera Arts* magazines and a columnist for *Photo Techniques* magazine and the Apple Web site. He teaches workshops and lectures extensively. To see his work and read several of his artists' statements, visit **www.johnpaul caponigro.com**. He wrote the Design Culture column, edited by Wendy Richmond.

Luke Sullivan came to WestWayne in 1998 after ten years at the well-regarded Minneapolis agency Fallon McElligott. Prior to that, he was a vice president at The Martin Agency in Richmond, Virginia. He began his career as an understudy of Tom McElligott at Bozell & Jacobs. His twenty years of experience includes work for such clients as Miller Lite beer, *Time* magazine, United Airlines, Lee Jeans, US West Communications and Ralston Purina, as well as Porsche and Maserati automobiles. At WestWayne, Luke personally oversees creative work on all accounts from all departments. He is the author of a book on advertising, *Hey Whipple, Squeeze This*, and has twice been named by *Adweek* magazine as one of the top ten copywriters in America. He has been honored in every national and international show, including London's D&AD, Cannes and *Communication Arts*, and has some twenty medals from The One Show. Luke enjoys the indoors and likes to spend a lot of his time there. He wrote the Advertising column, edited by Ernie Schenck.

Ruth Hagopian is a freelance designer and writer who specializes in digital art. She co-founded a San Francisco design firm, Visual Strategies, and was a contributing editor to *OnLine Design*, a publication for electronic art and graphics. Ruth wrote the Business column, and two book reviews.

Tad Crawford, the Legal/Business Affairs editor for *Communication Arts*, is the publisher of Allworth Press and author of *Legal Guide for the Visual Artist*, the *Business and Legal Forms* series for creative professionals, *The Secret Life of Money* and his most recent book, *The Money Mentor: A Tale of Finding Financial Freedom*.

Barbara Gordon, an artist and photographer representative since 1969, is a past president of the Society of Photographers and Artists Representatives and a member of the Society of Illustrators and the Graphic Artists Guild. She is also the author of two books: *Opportunities in Commercial Art and Graphic Design* (Vgm Career Horizons) and *How to Sell Your Art and Photography* (Writers Digest Books). She heads her own firm, Barbara Gordon Associates, in New York City, and has written on freelance issues for CA since 1982.

Dugald Stermer is an illustrator and author who wrote his first article for CA in 1966, and edited two issues of the magazine, in 1971 and 1980 respectively. He is the author of four books, the most recent being *Vanishing Flora* (Abrams, 1995). He is the chair of the illustration program at the California College of Arts & Crafts, and serves on the boards of The Illustrators' Partnership of America and The Illustration Conference. In addition, Dugald is a member of the San Francisco Arts Commission. He wrote an Opinion/Commentary piece in this issue.

Gary W. Priester is a New Mexico-based graphic designer, author and journalist. He is the author of *Looking Good in Color* (Ventana Press) and co-author of *CorelDRAW Studio Techniques* (Osborne/McGraw Hill). Priester worked for 25 years as an advertising art director before making the transitions to graphic design, where he is a principal in The Black Point Group, and then to writing. Priester is a regular contributor to **Efuse.com**, **GoBizGo.com**, **Designer.com**, **WebDevelopersJournal.com**, **Unleash.com** and other dot-coms. He is host of the XaraXone at **i-us.com** where he creates monthly tutorials in the Trompe L'Oeil Room for Xara X. Contact him at garypriester@earthlink.net. He contributed a software review for the REsources column, and wrote a book review.

Sam McMillan is a San Francisco-based writer, teacher and producer of interactive multimedia projects for a number of Bay Area production houses. He contributed to both the REsources and Book Reviews columns.

Book Reviews

Angelynn Grant is a Boston-based graphic designer, writer and educator. She has taught at Rhode Island School of Design, the Art Institute of Boston, Simmons College and MIT. Her freelance work ranges from compact discs to Web site design. You can e-mail her at inquiries@angelynngrant.com. In addition, Angelynn is the host of a jazz program on MIT radio, WMBR.

Canon Digital Creators Contest 2002

Step onto the world's stage with your digital imaging work
www.canon.com/cdcc/

© Katsura Moshino

Entries Now Accepted Worldwide   Gold Award: US$ 20,000

Entry Categories

■□□□ **Digital Photo (Print) Division** —— Photograph(s) captured with a digital camera; direct-print (unmodified) printout of a digitized photo(s); or printout of a digital camera image(s) that has been digitally modified

□■□□ **Digital Graphics /**
Illustration (Print) Division —— Printouts of computer-generated graphics, illustrations, etc.

□□■□ **Digital Movie Division** —— Modified and/or edited live-action digital movies shot with a digital video camcorder; or computer-graphics animated movies

□□□■ **Web Division** —————— Web-based graphics or other images (interactive or noninteractive) viewable over the Internet using Internet Explorer 5.0 (or later versions) or Netscape Navigator 4.7 (or later versions)

For official contest rules, please visit www.canon.com/cdcc/

For inquiries, contact:

Canon Digital Creators Contest
New York Secretariat

E-mail : info-us@c-dcc.com
Tel : 212-261-4200
Fax : 212-397-3322
URL : www.canon.com/cdcc/

Organized by: Canon Inc.
Sponsored by:
Adobe Systems Inc./Adobe Systems Co., Ltd., Benetton Group S.p.A./Benetton Japan Co., Ltd., Macromedia Inc./Macromedia Japan K.K., Canon Sales Co., Inc./Canon U.S.A., Inc./Canon Europa N.V./Canon Europe Ltd./Canon (China) Co., Ltd./Canon Singapore Pte. Ltd./Canon Hongkong Co., Ltd./Canon Australia Pty. Ltd.

Entry Period

Monday, April 1 – Tuesday, September 3, 2002
All entries must be received by 5:00 pm local time on September 3, 2002

Judges

Jeff Schewe (Photographer), tomato (Creative Unit, UK), Katsura Moshino (Illustrator/Art Director), Hiroyuki Nakano (Director), Scott Ross (CEO, President, and Co-founder of Digital Domain, Inc.), Joshua Davis (Artist / Technologist)
Special Judge: Ryuichi Sakamoto (Musician)
Contest Supervisor: Hiroshi Kashiwagi (Professor, Musashino Art University)

All the brand names are trademarks or registered trademarks of respective companies.

Letters to the Editor

"Illustration: Graphic Design's Poor Relation"

This article [Jan/Feb, p. 12] is a little irresponsible. Why would any one creative professional downgrade the importance of another? It's like the farmer criticizing the fertilizer supplier—how healthy is that for everyone? The article can be read different ways resulting in different perceptions by readers. Is it really for or against illustration? And again, why on earth would it be against?

The article's headline: Illustration: Graphic Design's Poor Relation, is unfortunately, for illustrators, a very damaging one-liner which carries more power than the entire article, given that many busy people will flip through the magazine looking at the pictures and pausing only for headlines. Clearly, this headline leaves a distinct impression on those not interested in the rest of the story—a firmly negative impression.

As an illustrator I don't feel slighted or hurt, I guess I feel a bit like illustration is left standing in a game of musical chairs; it's all in good fun I suppose, and I understand the humor in the article, but the chosen headline for this article was a very bad choice. No facet of the creative industry is doing so good that it can afford to be spoken of as, "_____ is a big fat idiot."

This is not an article that helps illustrators at all by way of that headline, no matter how funny or amusing its intent. How does it help design?

JOEL WILKINSON
GREENVILLE, SOUTH CAROLINA

Laurie Rosenwald responds: Firstly I would like to say that I am thrilled and delighted to have inspired much dissent, antagonism, and also staunch support among Communication Arts *readers. In addition, on Web sites such as theispot and IPA, my article provoked the following piece of vitriol:*

"Ms. Rosenwald's work appears to be little more than felt tip pen on cocktail napkin! This is not Art in any reasonable person's understanding of that exalted word, and she should cease and desist this instant! Because I said so! Reason enough I dare say! Harrumph!" —Anonymous

I responded to the courageous "Anonymous" by pointing out that I take great exception to its statement. I can also draw on paper towels, coffee filters and party hats.

As for Mr. Wilkinson's more thoughtful reaction, which represents objections repeated in many other letters, I can only reply that the title, "Illustration: Graphic Design's Poor Relation" was intended to stop readers in their tracks; if an individual was either too busy or uninterested to read on, so be it. I am not responsible for other people's reading habits. And by the way, America wouldn't merit defending if we couldn't point out that people are big fat idiots if we want to.

I stand by my words and my images. My Shakespeare book jacket that won an AIGA Fifty Books award was drawn on paper towel on a kitchen table. The only software I needed was my talent.

Almost all of these letters said something like "it's all in good fun I suppose, and I understand the humor in the article, but…"

Frankly, I don't agree. I think outraged illustrators who post cranky letters on illustrators' Web sites (I never even knew these existed before) are the most defensive bunch of crybabies it has ever been my privilege to provoke. Why are they so threatened? If I had written an article titled "Plumbers Are Vastly Inferior to Electricians," do you think it would have provoked anything but laughter? Could this outburst of indignation from the "Illustration Community" derive from the shock of recognition that the title inspires? I think they doth protesteth too mucheth. If you spot it, you got it.

Nowhere in the piece do I say that I think illustration is nothing; even when I say, "Admit it. Everybody knows that Illustration is nothing" I am commenting with irony (Heard of it?) on what I feel is the unspoken status of Illustration among others. I wanted to find out why this is. In schools where the Graphic Design department is separate from Illustration, it just seems to me that Illustration is looked down on. I don't think it should be a separate department in schools. It is a commercial application of drawing. Drawing is an essential tool for communication. For everybody. I worry about people who can't draw, only click. They make bad work that looks all alike, in my view. Whatever they call themselves, they're no good.

Another letter said, "I'd say hers is a view from the bottom looking up." Guess what? That's true. If I had more commercial success I probably wouldn't think the way I do.

But why would someone as successful as Brad Holland say, "I am Not An Illustrator"? I went to the Society of Illustrators Awards show the other day, where I met Brad Holland. Does he not represent the very apotheosis of success in Illustration? At one point he said to me: I am not an Illustrator. Why would he say that? I think it's because when you say "I am an Illustrator" it sounds limiting. But I might be wrong. I am often wrong! Then again, I am not deciding foreign policy.

Please Note: He didn't say that. I'm saying that. I would welcome his explanation.

Working on commission and making minute, idiotic changes seems, at least to me, a bad way to spend time. Maybe I'm the only one who has to make changes like: "Could you make the dog more Presbyterian? Can you make the pretzel saltier? Can you lace the sneakers? I guess it's just me. All those self-righteous yet oddly cranky illustrators said their work was so [CONTINUED ON PAGE 159]

Take a New Look | Fraser Papers

Capturing the nuances, depth and warmth of fine art portraiture demands the premium qualities found in Fraser Papers' Pegasus.

To receive a copy of *Portraits on Pegasus* featuring the work of fifteen internationally renowned photographers, call 800-543-3297 option 7 or contact your local Fraser Papers merchant.

marketingservices@fraserpapers.com

Letters to the Editor

creative, so self-determined, so respected. Clearly, my assumptions are all wrong. Again. So if I'm all wrong, why get mad? Lighten up!

I've been teaching since 1979. I've been working for the past year on New York Notebook, *which Chronicle will publish next Spring. I wrote it, I Illustrated it, I designed it. I designed a typeface for Font Bureau (Loupot). I worked as a freelance editorial designer for the* New York Times *and* Condé Nast *for fourteen years. I have had success as a comic. I recently had an exhibition of paintings at the H55 Gallery in New York and have a short story coming out in the next* Thurber House Collection of American Humor. *So when I am called an illustrator, yes, it bugs me. OK?*

Another criticism of my article needs to be addressed. Some believed my article reinforced a bias against Illustration by CA. I don't speak for anybody but Laurie Rosenwald. The subject was not their idea. If there was any "agenda" on their part by publishing it, I was unaware of it. Also, the editor's note at the end of the piece I will not repeat here, but it does not represent an accurate "summing up" of my own feelings as expressed in the article, and I didn't know about it until it was printed.

Right On Rosenwald

Right on…but you're preaching to the converted. I wonder if any young minds will absorb this…I suspect a few.

"All mature artists and designers draw on a wide variety of tools to communicate and technology sometimes makes it easier to do so. Sometimes they make it too easy, and then things get really ugly."

This rang so true to me. My canvas these days is mostly digital and displayed on the Web. On the Web, where design/illustration runs amuck…it sometimes seems so hollow and the ugliness you describe permeates. But, there are good illustrations and when I

see them, their work shines through the mess.

Anyway, thanks for sharing your thoughts—I enjoyed reading them.

TOM WOLFE
CANADA

Offenbach's Photos

I am surprised that you included John Offenbach's photos for American Airlines [March/April, p. 54] that now conjure up images of September 11 terrorists attacks. I was in New York on that day and I don't wish to be reminded. Weren't there other images from his portfolio that you could have used?

DANA LYNN DREINHOFER
MANGER PUBLICATION SERVICES
UNIVERSITY OF WYOMING
LARAMIE, WYOMING

Rick Colby

Sonuvagun! I'm flipping through my CA [March/April, p. 76] and I see these neat ads for California Avocados, California Pizza Kitchen, and Oolong Tea. I'm thinking to myself, this is good stuff. I've always liked the California-driven ads, being a native (the California Cooler surfing spots from the early '80s are still my all-time winner being a surfer myself!). Then I start to read the article and I'm looking at this guy and he looks oh-so-familiar. Why, it's Rick Colby! My classmate from San Jose State! The same Rick Colby that sold print services in New York before seeing the light and moving West, buying a Fiat 124 Spyder, growing his beard, and being one of the best copywriters to ever emerge from the hallowed halls of SJSU. He's done well. And, if I'm not mistaken, I think he had something to do with the AMD "Catch the Wave" spots where a guy was surfing in a suit

way back in the mid '80s. Kudos to Rick. May the California lifestyle continue to flourish!

And a small cheer for the San Jose State ad program. Cowabunga!

JIM LUCAS
SR. MANAGER OF MARKETING
    COMMUNICATIONS
AMCC
SUNNYVALE, CALIFORNIA

Olympic Winter Games of 2002

Does an Olympic Game design process need to have controversy and back stabbing in order to get more than five pages of editorial these days? I'm thinking of past features on Atlanta and Los Angeles. I've subscribed for over twenty years and recall much more informative reviews of the comprehensive process of design for previous Olympics, as compared to the skinny article on Salt Lake's Winter Games in your March/April issue [p. 99]. I would have enjoyed seeing some of Joel Nakamura's illustrations reproduced larger than a postage stamp, and an extended article about the design firms involved. Not only is this one of the key assignments in one's career for our profession, it happens so infrequently it deserves deeper coverage.

Matthew Porter's article seemed like it could have run in *USA Today*, where short attention spans are the norm. This story should have been the main feature of this issue, with two or three less uninspiring *Exhibit* features.

TERRI O'HARE
O'HARE COMMUNICATIONS, INC.
VERO BEACH, FLORIDA

Letters to the Editor

[Anja Kroencke, March/April, p. 14]
For someone who is so obviously irate

Letters to the Editor

for having their work plagiarized, and accusatory toward *Communication Arts* for not recognizing it, I'm amused (amazed?) Anja has such little understanding of the judging process she so freely criticizes, condemns the magazine that publishes her work so she may boast to being "as established as I," but yet has not a single vitriolic word for the thief!

"…one would expect, if not demand, that *Communication Arts* would be sensitive to the issue of copyright infringement." (My God Tad, how many articles have you written in CA over the years!)

In regard to another quote "*Communication Arts* itself had described my work as instantly-recognizable." Was this a collective quote from the entire staff of CA? Of course not! Of Jean Coyne, or Patrick Coyne or one of the many Contributing Editors? Probably.

Her work may be recognizable to the person who made that statement, but it seems a bit over the top to think the entire graphics industry recognizes her work. (I don't!)

She would be more appreciative if CA took an interest in the qualifications of their juries. How? Ask everyone if they "recognize" her work? Has she not read the bios of the panel of judges? Did she notice that they are all practicing professionals in their craft. Many with their own studios, agencies and most of them nationally and internationally recognized for their own work?

"…it is not too much to expect that the jury of *Communication Arts* would at least have a passing familiarity with the art featured on the pages of its own magazine." Not one judge—ever— has been asked; "Do you subscribe to *Communication Arts* and are you familiar with the published works of the last xyz issues? The judges are selected for their diversity (To give a diverse flavor to the selection of the winning entries!)

and maybe—just maybe—coming from all points of the country, some being illustrators/designers/photographers themselves, some being corporate clients, some being art directors, some of them don't recognize her work. (Horrors!)

As I said at the beginning, it doesn't seem she has a beef with the thief, but rather how shabbily she's been treated by *Communication Arts*. I would suggest you invite her to be a judge so she can see the incredible integrity that has gone into 43+ years developing the very best process of judging the largest showcase of work in the world.

Then, she will recognize her diatribe for the sour grapes that it is.

KURT KLEIN
SENIOR PRODUCTION MANAGER
AUSTIN, TEXAS

Deliver Us From Web Art

Stop! Drop the JPEG and step away. This is almost the stance that we designers must take in order to ensure our work doesn't fall in with a bad, pixelated crowd.

I have noticed an increasingly disturbing trend in using pixelated, over sharpened images in magazines, catalogs and other usually high-quality publications…and it's somehow acceptable. These images are apparently used for lack of anything better. Have we lost our minds? Why do we allow this sort of trash to proliferate? Have we forgotten that as a general rule, Web-ready images are not acceptable for print? I have this problem just as much as any designer. Clients who have no concept of the difference between a 72PPI JPEG and a 300DPI TIFF submit anything they can find for imagery. This usually means that they scour the Internet for something relevant to their piece and then proudly submit it like it is a Rembrandt. Admittedly, I take guilty pleasure in telling them that their photos

are unusable then set about explaining to them the difference between 300DPI and 72PPI because they were too impatient to listen the first time. When I come back to earth, I realize that all this wasted time and effort was my fault for not forcing them to listen to why Internet images just won't work. Let's wake up, people!

We are the only ones who can stop this disgusting degradation of our efforts. We must make it a point to educate those who don't understand what it takes to do proper design. We can not allow this to go on. If we do, we have no place criticizing bad design, for we are all responsible. Let's make the world safe for good design again and uphold the values that we learned in art school. Bless the Web and bless print, just don't let them play together. We all have seen what happens when you do.

CHRISTIAN ANDREW SIBLEY
GRAPHIC DESIGNER
SHREWSBURY, PENNSYLVANIA

Recycle

As I've noticed on your packaging the following note:

PLEASE RECYCLE THIS MAILER CREATIVELY

Why don't you hold a contest for your subscribers on how they DO creatively recycle them—it would be great fun!

JANE WREDE
ART DIRECTOR
MILWAUKEE, WISCONSIN

Address correspondence to: Letters to the Editor, 110 Constitution Drive, Menlo Park, California 94025 or e-mail letters@commarts.com. We reserve the right to publish letters and to edit for clarity and length. Please include a signature, address and phone number. Anonymous letters will not be published.

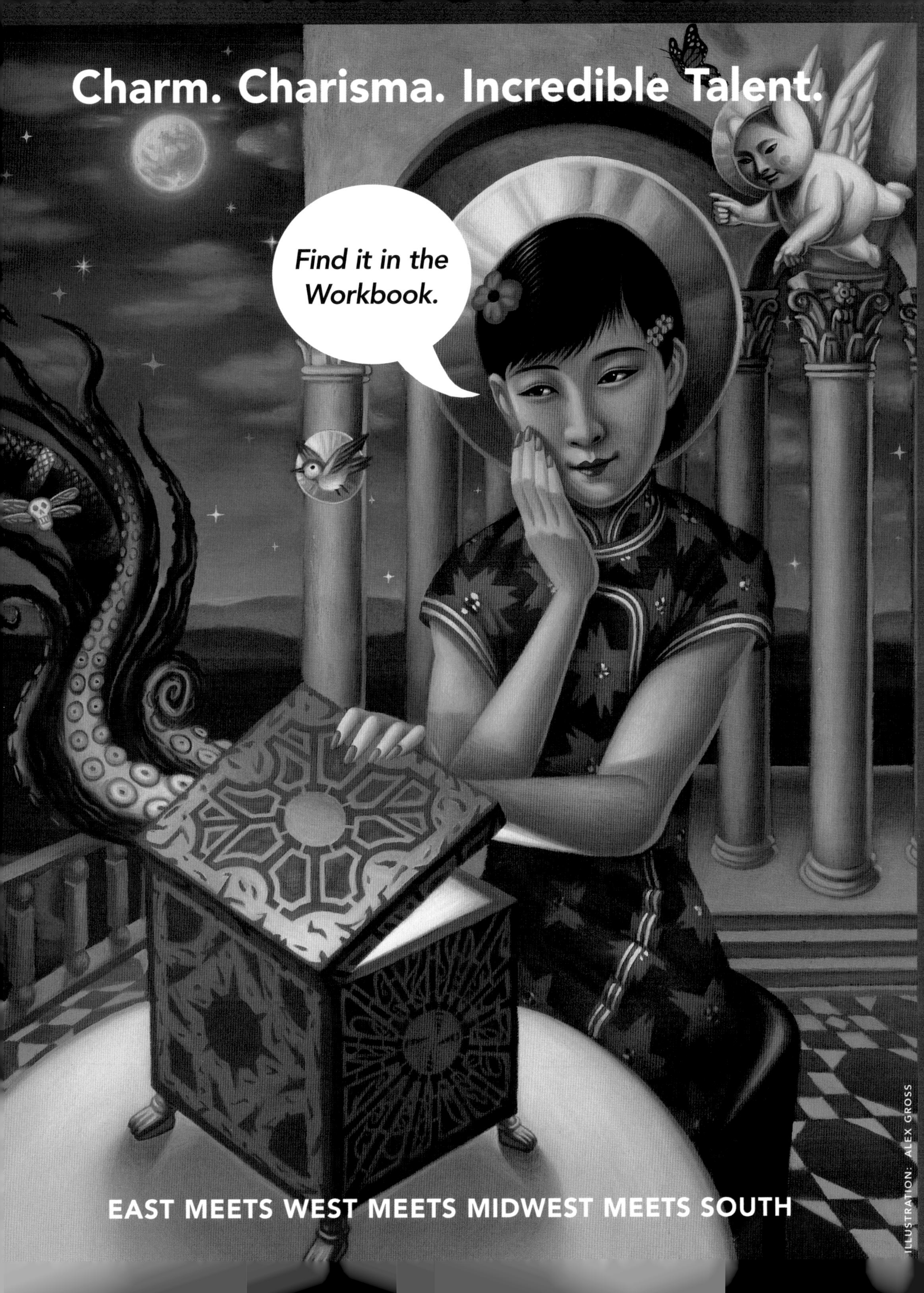

ILLUSTRATION: ALEX GROSS

Charles Glaubitz

Location: "La Linea/The Border" inside the paradox of Tijuana, Baja California, and San Diego, California.

Duration: I have been illustrating off and on since I began going to school about three or four years now. I recently graduated from CCAC, so it's been a year-and-a-half non stop.

Staff: One.

Education: Associate degree San Diego City College graphic design 1998; certificate Rafael López Illustration Workshop 1997; B.F.A. illustration California College of Arts and Crafts, San Francisco 2001; and probably the most important part, my apprenticeship with illustrator extraordinare Rafael López.

Cultural Influences: Hybridity. Father German-American from Nebraska/mother Mexican from Los Mochis Sinaloa. It is reflected in the hybridity between the two cities that I live in (San Diego/Tijuana). My work is also a hybrid of the reflection of the cultural duality that utilizes and combines iconography, symbols, metaphors, allegories, stealing, discarding, experimenting with images from "La Linea." Also lowbrow art, the subculture, comic books, art, anime, manga.

Environment: Home studio in Playas de Tijuana and in Visual Asylum (San Diego). I share time and space with great people in both places (I am lucky).

Philosophy: Visual narrative…intuition, honesty, imagination, observation are the secrets for creativity…hybridity is the result of the sum of two differences…duality is as simple as day and night…do everything you do in life for the righteous cause of love, that's the secret for life.

1. *El Mañanero*, part of a group show, *Just Say No*, at the Upper Playground Gallery in San Francisco. It's about the pros and cons of marijuana usage. Acrylic on wood.

2. *Robocat* used in the 2002 Outer Space calendar. Mark Murphy, art director; Murphy Design, design firm.

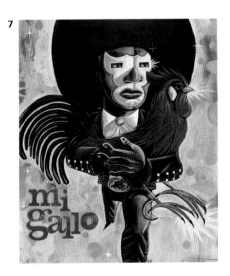

3. *Color Birds* for the AIGA San Diego "Tweet Street." Amy Levine/Maelin Levine, art directors; Visual Asylum, design firm. Digital.

4. *La Sirena, Birth of a Sea Monkey*. Group exhibition at La Luz de Jesus Gallery. Acrylic on canvas.

5. *Lonely Astronaut*. Personal piece about the pursuit of humans reinventing technology into nature. In the process, we have become disconnected from our own nature and enclosed ourselves in technology in the pursuit of making it our nature. Acrylic on wood.

6. *Santa Land Diaries*. Llance Bower, art director; Old Globe Theatres, client.

7. *Mi Gallo*, part of the *Guapo y Fuerte* exhibition at Anno Domini gallery in San Jose. Mark Murphy, art director/curator.

Kenny Johnson

Location: 400 E. 17th, Kansas City, Missouri 64108.

Duration: Around five years.

Staff: Two.

Education: Associate Degree in commercial art, Mom, Dad, Michael Rush (my mentor).

Cultural Influences: I feel like my life is culture. Everything you touch, see and feel are really the things that make you who you are. (God, family, music, film, cartoon Friday, magazines, just life.)

Environment: I think it's amazing how much you can learn from just doing the things you do, constantly re-honing the skills that you may already possess. Mostly, I see my work space as a relatively calm place to do work, photographically communicate solutions in hopefully what are appropriate terms for that particular situation. Words to describe the environment: energetic, peaceful, calm, fun.

Philosophy: If you build it, they will come.

1

2

1. *Angie*.

2. *Paul's House*.

3. *Yeah Baby*. Sheri Terranova/Kevin Garrison, art directors; Lisa Weaver, stylist; Beauty Brands, client.

4. *Have You Seen My Bag?*

5. *Eric & Misty*.

6. *Love You, Love You Too*. Sheri Terranova/Kevin Garrison, art directors; Lisa Weaver, stylist; Beauty Brands, client.

7. *Danielle*. Lisa Weaver, stylist.

delux design associates

Location: Burlington, Vermont, U.S.A.

Duration: Three-plus years.

Staff: In-house staff of three, plus a variety of collaborators including illustrators, photographers, designers, copywriters and other artists. We also normally have any number of interns milling about.

Education: Karalyn McManiman Middings, CEO, co-founder, B.A. in mass communications from Penn State University; Keith Brown, chief creative officer, co-founder, B.F.A. in graphic design from Maine College of Art; Heather Madison Drury, senior art director, B.F.A. in graphic design from SUNY Fredonia.

Cultural Influences: Abba, *Adbusters*, Ben Bagdikian, *Blade Runner*, Calvin, cheap cameras, Noam Chomsky, chrome, cinema, The Clash, Leonard Cohen, cool stickers, Designers Republic, DIY, '80s one-hit wonders, feng shui, flowers, 43, found objects, The Fresh Market, french fries, Peter Gabriel's "Passion", Massive Attack, Henri Matisse, metallic ink, the *New York Times Magazine*, Georgia O'Keefe, Vaughan Oliver, origami, Daniel Quinn, round paper clips, *Sesame Street*, silk-screen posters, Swiss design, 12, veggie booty, Andy Warhol, Frank Lloyd Wright, yoga/meditation.

Environment: A self-designed studio in the creative mecca of Burlington, Vermont—open space with minimal divisions, which fosters communication, conversation and good foosball games. We host quarterly art exhibits showing work from distinctive artists, which keeps our studio both visually inspiring and constantly changing.

Philosophy: "A graphic design studio providing bold creative solutions to communication needs." We bring a high level of distinction and originality to each project, plus a level of marketing savvy that provides visually-unique solutions that are appropriate for each client's needs. We build long-term client relationships by developing clear brand-building solutions.

1

2

3

4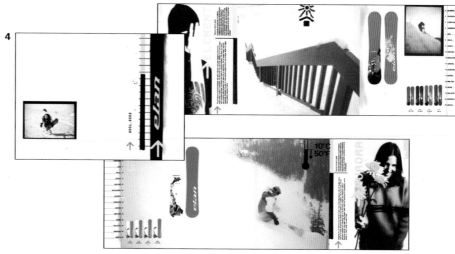

1. The Playwright is an Irish pub, and their previous logo didn't carry any heritage with it. Keith Brown, art director/designer.

2. Freeskiing Nationals poster. We tried to create a ski event poster that would stand out from the ubiquitous "blue sky" skier photo and copy. Keith Brown, art director/designer; Karalyn Middings, production manager.

3. Antique & Classic Car Show poster. A pro-bono, 2-color poster. Keith Brown, art director; Tim Clayton, designer; Karalyn Middings, production manager.

4. Elan snowboard catalog. We built upon the lifestyle and cultural elements of snowboarding. Keith Brown, art director; Keith Brown/Tim Clayton/Heather Drury, designers; Michael Sipe (portraits)/various (action), photographers; Christopher Middings, copyeditor; Karalyn Middings, production manager.

5. Line Mothership twin-tip powder skis. With industrial photography, we aimed for the antithesis of the typical backcountry ski graphic. Keith Brown, art director; Keith Brown/Tim Clayton, designers.

6. Line Darkside skis. A very hand-drawn, deep and raw composition, this illustration was art-directed in a style much looser than the artist normally works. Keith Brown, art director/designer; Patricia Middings, illustrator.

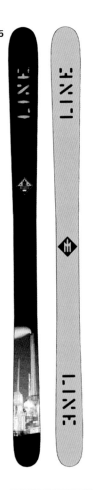

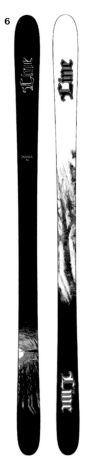

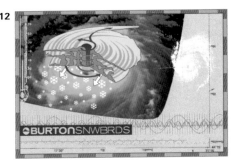

7. Elan Squid snowboard. An energetic illustration and subject for this junior snowboard graphic. Keith Brown, art director/illustrator; Keith Brown/Tim Clayton, designers.

8. Elan Element snowboard. For Elan's high-end freestyle board, we moved away from geometric graphics and towards more of a punk feel. Keith Brown, art director; Tim Clayton, designer/illustrator.

9. For the Line ad campaign, we had three goals: make the skier the hero, build a personality around them and create an honest ad relating to the core freeskiing skier. Keith Brown, art director; Tim Clayton, designer.

10. Line Skis Five-0 logo. Keith Brown, art director; Tim Clayton, designer.

11. Technology Consultants logo. Keith Brown, art director; Heather Drury/Keith Brown, designers.

12. Burton clothing tag. We were given instructions to illustrate the names with weather- and map-themed illustrations (Access, Tempest, AK) for their line of clothing. Keith Brown, art director; Keith Brown/Tim Clayton, designers.

13. Liquid Todd *Action* CD sleeve, in collaboration with Capacitor Design Network. Keith Brown, art director/designer.

You make the meaning. We make the means.

Fine Coated Papers   **Centura**   Productolith   **Fortune**

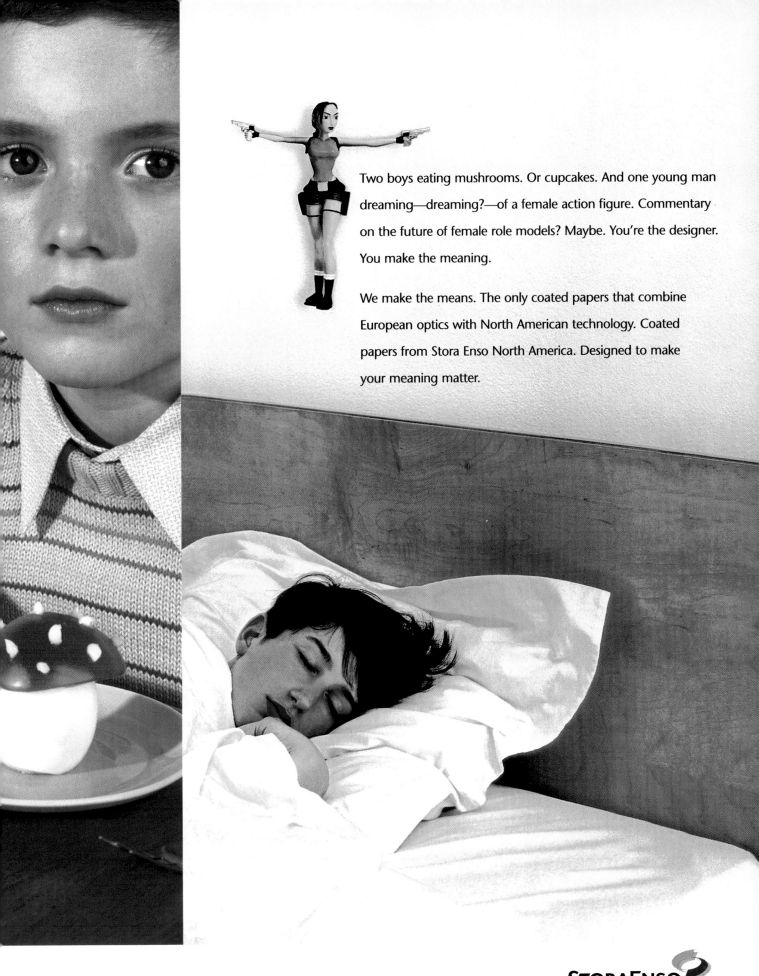

Two boys eating mushrooms. Or cupcakes. And one young man dreaming—dreaming?—of a female action figure. Commentary on the future of female role models? Maybe. You're the designer. You make the meaning.

We make the means. The only coated papers that combine European optics with North American technology. Coated papers from Stora Enso North America. Designed to make your meaning matter.

The Designer Is Dead, Long Live the Designer

BY ROGER WHITEHOUSE

Many years ago in a city far, far away—London, actually, in the winter of 1959—I made my way home from my studio at the Architectural Association in Bedford Square where I had worked late into the night on a student project. While passing through the swirling fog into Soho Square, past doorways where leather-mini-skirted ladies dispensed sultry winks and double-entendred invitations, my attention was drawn to a basement store. Two young men stood in an isolated pool of light animatedly discussing a pale blue sheet of paper that was covered with row after row of characters from the alphabet. My attention was riveted. In those days, the sight of typographic characters liberated from the forbidden sanctuary of the printshop was even more tempting than Soho's more lascivious delights.

I discovered that these two men, Fred Mackenzie and Di Davies, (not mentioned in any formal histories) held in their hands one of the apocalyptic developments that would play its part in the transformation of the practice of graphic design. They had just invented and patented Letraset, in those days a quaint process which involved characters screened onto a glue-covered sheet of paper creating transfers which when cut out, dropped into warm water, and placed on the under surface of a tiny silk screen, could be positioned over a piece of artwork to be popped down into place with the poke of a finger. *Anyone's* finger.

In the months to come, the innocent looking sheets began to appear first in design studios and then, horror of horrors, as the process evolved into the more familiar rub-down format, on the desks of secretaries and clerks and political activists and pensioners and schoolchildren and even the ladies in Soho Square. The more exotic the typeface (and this was the dawn of the 1960s), the more delighted these new typographers became. Spacing was totally random, and the fashion of aligning the descenders of "g"s and "y"s and so on, on the same wavering approximation of a baseline on which the rest of the characters sat, became habitual. As the shredded sheets became depleted of certain characters, first inverted "d"s replaced "p"s, then capitals replaced lower case letters in the middle of words, and last and best of all, letters of different sizes from entirely different alphabets were imported to finish the job off.

The introduction of presstype introduced a whole new unintentional aesthetic which abandoned every accepted principle of typography.

Graphic designers everywhere tut-tutted and raised their eyebrows in superior disdain, but very few suspected that what they were observing were the seeds of their downfall. For years they had been the guardians of a secret realm; they were among the few cognoscenti who possessed the magic to turn handwritten words or typewritten manuscript into actual printed type. And it was this miraculous metamorphosis, revered as though it were akin to alchemy, that most mystified and impressed clients—together with all the tangential references to kerning, ligatures, picas and the rest of the arcane gobbledegook which enabled designers to sustain their mystique. But now the genie was squeezing out of the bottle. Typography was becoming a democratic endeavor, available for any Tom, Dick or Harriet to explore.

It turned out not to be such a severe threat at the time. After an initial flirtation with a sheet of rub-down Blippo Bold, most of these new typographers got bored and decided to let the graphic designers and printers wrestle with the stuff instead. But a subtle change was in fact taking place. A few of these new interlopers who were æsthetically astute enough began to make some graphic headway, unhindered by the conventions that restrained the traditional typographers, and together with the new liberation of the emerging '60s, began to create funky mischievous graphics of varying levels of sophistication which were photocopied and sent through the mail or taped to light poles and vacant storefronts everywhere.

This might all have passed unnoticed or at least have had little influence on the natural order of things were it not for the widespread arrival of offset lithography. In the very early twentieth century, those graphic designers who wanted to shake things up a bit, such as the Futurists, were still hamstrung by having to commandeer a printshop, and, with the owner presumably gagged and tied to a stool, jam type of all sizes at wacky angles into a form to be printed in the conventional manner, resulting in something which—while absolutely wonderful—strongly resembled a dysfunctional type specimen book. However, these early typographic revolutionaries were kept safely under control by the sheer complications involved—which remained beyond the patience of most decent God-fearing folk. It was not until

beau·ty *n.*

(1) pleasing and impressive qualities: the combination of qualities that make something pleasing and impressive, especially to look at.
(2) Graphistock photography

Graphistock *a division of Images.com, Inc.*
*16 West 19th Street New York NY 10011 **t** 1-800-4-IMAGES (1-800-446-2437) **f** 212-691-6609 **e** information@graphistock.com*
www.images.com

offset lithography came to flower in the post-war years, that this kind of experimentation became not only possible, but a breeze, by making feasible the printing of anything that could be drawn or pasted together on a sheet of paper.

But still, the potential of this new process to fully democratize graphic design was harnessed by the difficulties presented by the need for generating proper type in quantity. While headlines and even snappy little ads or flyers could be and often were put together by the use of presstype, body copy still had to be created by a strange hybrid process where it was set in metal, and final galleys or "repros" were pasted down onto boards to create mechanicals to be photographed to create plates for the offset presses. Thus, the sacred domain of designers and typographers still remained reasonably impregnable.

In the late 1980s the personal computer made its appearance. This time, we were totally fooled, welcoming this Trojan Horse with innocent delight. And why not? It

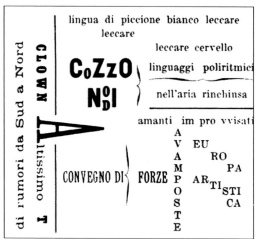

The Futurists experimented using metal type within the confines of the traditional printshop, predating the excesses made possible by rub-downs or computers.

made life much easier for us. We could actually, with our fancy new PostScript Laserwriters, generate type directly without the messy back and forth of galleys covered with proofreaders' marks and "move this to the right 1/100th em," and "enlarge all punctuation 12.5%." (I still hold the record for most author's alterations on a single project according to Tom Fischer of Typogram in New York, one of whose markup-infested galleys are still displayed in a frame in our office.)

Best of all, using computers really impressed clients then and if anything, boosted our mystique several notches. This was not surprising, as coaxing moderately respectable type from an early Macintosh (in one of all of ten fonts) demanded a skill level possessed only by the likes of Wernher von Braun.

Sadly, we were all too busy playing with our new toys to notice that when Apple described the Macintosh as a "computer for the rest of us," they knew what they were talking about. In very short order "the rest of us"—specifically our clients—also had snazzy new

Great illustrators represent **Gerald & Cullen Rapp**

Beth Adams

Philip Anderson

N. Ascencios

Daniel Baxter

Stuart Briers

Jonathan Carlson

R. Gregory Christie

Jack Davis

Robert de Michiell

The Dynamic Duo

Randall Enos

Leo Espinosa

Phil Foster

Mark Fredrickson

Chris Gall

Eliza Gran

Gene Greif

Tomer Hanuka

Peter Horjus

David Hughes

Celia Johnson

Douglas Jones

James Kaczman

J.D. King

Laszlo Kubinyi

Scott Laumann

Davy Liu

PJ Loughran

Bernard Maisner

Hal Mayforth

David McLimans

Aaron Meshon

James O'Brien

John Pirman

Marc Rosenthal

Alison Seiffer

Seth

Whitney Sherman

James Steinberg

Drew Struzan

Elizabeth Traynor

Anders Wenngren

Michael Witte

Noah Woods

Brad Yeo

And **Gerald & Cullen Rapp** has represented great illustrators since 1944

108 East 35th Street, New York, NY 10016 | Phone 212 889 3337 | Fax 212 889 3341 | www.theispot.com/rep/rapp

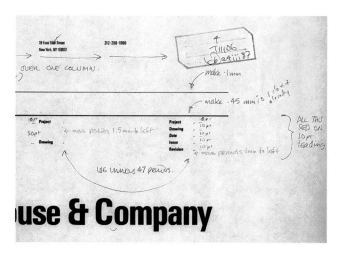

use & Company

Before the introduction of computers, the designers' ability to achieve finely tuned results required a constant ping-pong of elaborately marked up galleys between them and the typesetter.

computers (albeit made by another upstart company) that could also take that page of typewritten manuscript and pop it out in 12-point Helvetica. The writing was now on the wall—where it could easily be photographed and printed by offset lithography. The pieces of the puzzle began to fall into place and the final storming of our bastion began.

We all know that graphic design is much more than the ability to generate information in the form of nicely formatted typography. But that other stuff that we do, the important stuff—like having good concepts, turning ideas and information into something that sings, and employing a subtler visual rhetoric than gold foil-stamped starbursts, is not the first thing our clients worry about in a panic when they wake up at two o-clock in the morning. Instead, they go downstairs for a belt of Scotch, and in an insomniac furor, turn on their PCs, and have a go at the brochure that they had intended calling us about in the morning—just to see what all those words might actually look like in Times Roman. Then they add a picture or two, and try the odd rule here and there, and suddenly it begins to fit all the parameters that, in their minds, are required of an actual brochure. It may well be that in the clear light of dawn they have second thoughts and call us anyway, but all they need us to do now is just to "tidy it up a bit," and how much skill, fee or professional respect could that possibly demand?

If this assault on our prestige and pride were not bad enough, another change in public taste was underway that was not about to help our case. As typography slipped out of our exclusive control, liberties equal to those that Letraset had made possible twenty years before began to emerge and blossom. This time a new inelegance materialized of constantly varying type sizes, weights, styles and line lengths, with no apparent relationship to content, all peppered with dingbats and electronic clip art. The arrival of the World Wide Web added glows, starfields and stuttering animation

to all this, resulting in a wild ride into a world of visual chaos that would have made even a Futurist wince. While some clients may have noticed this was not quite as classy as the sort of thing Paul Rand or Brad Thompson used to do, most of the public have simply accepted it as the current yardstick of graphic excellence. Most significantly, the number of people who can nowadays discern the difference between the good, the bad, and the downright ugly is becoming depressingly small.

Thus, in the short span of a quarter of a century, not only what we do but how we do it has lost its lustre in the public eye. Not only are we in the process of losing our reputation as visionaries and artists, but we are in danger of accepting this new role and becoming simply a bunch of visual mechanics.

Part and parcel with this is a change in how we are relating to each other as professionals. Twenty-five years ago, when I defected from architecture into graphic design, it was a very different profession. I was introduced to, and welcomed by, a world of legendary individuals like Massimo and Lela Vignelli, Tom Geismar and Ivan Chermayeff, and Colin Forbes, all virtuosos of both their art and their craft. I will never forget one afternoon when as a relative newcomer, I dropped in on Massimo unannounced. While I am sure he was desperately busy, he graciously took me by the arm and with his usual charm gave me a guided tour around his entire studio, storerooms included. These designers were passionate about what they did and how they did it, and were exceptionally generous in sharing what they knew, even their advice on business practices, with aspiring newcomers. At board meetings of AIGA, of which I became a director, I was aware of a rich and established culture of dedicated individuals for whom design was a lifelong passion and where all of us felt we were in the vanguard of important change. On a conscious and unconscious level it was a political as well as a creative culture, dedicated to making the world more fun, more thoughtful and more decent.

Today, the demise of the designer as an expert and visionary—because of the cheap availability of what now passes for design—has seen the introduction of a bottom line-oriented profession where designers are becoming more focused on being pragmatic businesspeople than on being idealists. I mourn the passing of the established culture—and while I see it as just the inevitable collateral damage of progress, something which we must react and respond to—we face an urgent need to redirect our profession and evolve values which work in the context of current realities.

Sadly, the effect on some design firms, particularly the larger and more prominent ones, is that in an attempt to keep the company coffers full (or to stop them emptying any further), they appear to be rapidly losing touch with the inspiration that built their reputations, becoming instead caught up in the Faustian desperation of having to concen-

Martini glass removed by KnockOut 2.
Olive removed by someone who doesn't like olives.

Hate olives? Get rid of them. Hate complex masking? Get KnockOut 2. Separate objects from their backgrounds, and still preserve elements like transparency and fine details. So masking things like smoke, glass, hair, and of course liquids, is now completely possible. KnockOut 2 is also a compatible plug-in to Adobe® Photoshop® for seamless workflow. Stirred your curiosity? Visit us at www.procreate.com for more information.

procreate™

trate on feeding the beast they have sold their souls to. The old professional camaraderie is becoming anathema to their need to compete for both projects and staff with designers who were once their creative and professional allies.

The decay of these professional values is a serious problem because it is very important that as a profession we make the public aware of the value of design, and it is only as an orchestrated group that we can do this. Our professional institutions still concentrate on preaching to the choir, with pat-ourselves-on-the-back design shows rather than promoting serious discourse about our professional predicament. A colleague recently suggested that the reason we continually give ourselves awards is because no one else will (this, and the fact that the design institutions have learned that the way to our pocketbooks is through our egos). It is not so much that the design shows are bad, they are just irrelevant.

Educating our clients will not be easy. To do so, we must first thoroughly understand what it is that we do, and what the specific values of that are, and to whom, and in what way. Unfortunately, most designers have little if any concern with this, being obsessed with "look how clever I am" stuff. We must also be wary. While the need to educate our clients is important, we must avoid the impulse to do so in an attempt to turn back the clock to the good old days. If clients no longer value us very much, it is neither a moral issue or necessarily a deficiency on their part. It is an inevitability brought about by a whole confluence of reasons, many of which we must bear the responsibility for. We must primarily think of this as our "problem," not theirs. Designer, heal thyself. After we have successfully done that, prescribing a stiff remedy for our clients may then have some validity.

What of the future? Almost certainly even more of the same. The rapid development of direct-to-plate digital printing and high-speed inkjet presses, where ever smaller runs in full color can be generated directly from anyone's computer files at ever decreasing cost, have eliminated the need for the prep work that had become the printer's stock-in-trade. The new technologies are migrating to ever smaller desktop units where both printer and printshop alike will be rendered entirely redundant for those projects which do not involve complex binding or other manufacturing demands, and it may not be long before some ingenious individual domesticates even this last preserve of their trade. Add to this the rapidly developing effectiveness of the Web to accomplish sales, distribution and fulfillment, and it is easy to see that any individual with the right entrepreneurial spirit can create an entire publishing empire from their bedroom (although they may not get much sleep).

Not that it should make us feel any better, but the same is true of the other creative professions. Anyone with a new iMac, a video camera, a copy of iMovie and the talent, can produce a broadcastable movie from start to finish, including burning and labeling the DVD, for an equipment cost of less than $3,000. For $10,000 they can do the same thing of fairly decent broadcast quality. And music, photography and most of the other "media"-based arts have seen similar reshaping of their professional environments.

The first thing graphic designers are challenged to do is to distinguish themselves again, perhaps by developing new æsthetics based more upon the raw energy of concept and message, than just relying on elegantly kerned type. While energy of concept and message were what our mentors, like Massimo, were very adept at in a polite and polished way, whippersnapper designers, like Stefan Sagmeister, have shown us how this can work in a more visceral way, in his case with arresting and often disturbing images (frequently miscellaneous body parts) surrounded by handwritten copy. You can still have that elegant Vignelli kerning if you want to, but take a look at the latest version of Adobe InDesign and while you drool on the keyboard watch it, with none of

I mourn the passing of the established culture—and while I see it as just the inevitable collateral damage of progress, something which we must react and respond to—we face an urgent need to redirect our profession and evolve values which work in the context of current realities.

your hard-earned expertise, take a page of type, re-rag it from top to bottom, apply optical kerning, hang any punctuation and automatically insert ligatures—probably even better than you can.

Beyond all this is the further challenge to take control of the projects we work on by becoming more entrepreneurial and instead of giving our ideas away for the financial benefit of others, to retain control and ownership of what we do and exploit and earn from it directly. In a climate where we are being continually devalued, taking charge of our own fate also has the potential to garner back some of the stature and respect we are losing—not just to soothe bruised egos, but to enjoy the freedom to be heard and express ourselves.

Tibor Kalman was a notable pioneer of both of these avenues of opportunity. I remember several years ago being with Tibor at a very exclusive club on Manhattan's Upper East Side where we had been invited to a rather posh fundraiser. On being confronted with a large chafing dish full of french fries, he stuffed handfuls of them into every pocket. He then proceeded around the room and after insinuating himself into each little bejeweled and evening-gowned

DigitAllart

Make your bright ideas even brighter. The Samsung 1200NF.

Now there's a clear translation from thought to screen. With the 1200NF you'll experience razor sharp clarity. An undistorted view from any angle. Bold, saturated colors. No wonder so many serious graphic designers choose Samsung to bring their vision to life.

- 20" Viewable Area
- 2048 x 1536 @ 75 Hz Maximum Resolution
- Natural Flat .24mm Uni-Pitch Aperture Grille
- Dual CPU Selectable Video Inputs

See where your ideas go with the 1200NF.

Not just digital... Samsung DigitAll!

To learn more about the Samsung SyncMaster 1200NF and other monitors visit us at **www.samsungusa.com**

900NF 210T 240T

© 2002 Samsung Electronics America, Inc.

SAMSUNG DIGITall
everyone's invited™

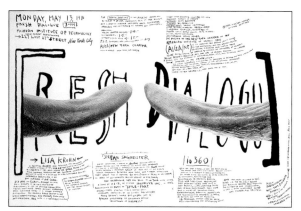

Both these posters derive their vigor and clarity from vivid concepts, the first, by Vignelli Associates in a formal way, reflecting the tradition of carefully crafted type, while the second, by Stefan Sagmeister, uses raw imagery and informal handwritten copy.

M&Co went beyond the traditions of graphic design with a strong entrepreneurial spirit, creating and marketing among a host of other items, these typically Tiborian paperweights.

huddle of guests, suddenly pulled fries out of one pocket or another and proffered them with such determined innocence that the amazed guests took them and munched away in stunned silence. This was a perfect metaphor for what Tibor did with design, ignoring the hygiene of elegant typography and relying instead on the raw energy of concept. Of course it was not that what his firm M&Co ended up with was in any way design-deficient, it just invented its own laws of æsthetics as it went along. This, plus the utter conviction of everything it did was the key to its success. The other path that is open to us is that of design entrepreneur, also well trodden by Tibor, who like some magician at a kids' party, pulled a seemingly inexhaustible progression of watches and paperweights and clocks, and all kinds of neat stuff that he had designed and had manufactured, out of thin air.

The challenge now to the profession, particularly for the schools, is to develop a generation of designers more heavily focused on taking the lead in the development of projects rather than on just providing design services; designers who have a first-class cultural education, are savvy, and are entrepreneurial; more able to develop concepts for products for which there is a market, and to make their money by holding on to the rights of those properties. There will still be a decent market for service design, particularly for higher end corporate and institutional print and Web work, but the level of taste is diminishing, and designers are being perceived as much lesser players and will have much less control than they may be comfortable with. Within conventional design, the new technologies will hopefully give designers more time to focus on a more

This simply and elegantly-produced trade paperback, written by Steve Martin, and designed by Richard Oriello, is a refreshing example of everyday design at its best: A clear concept, well executed, and with the general public, not some select insiders, as its audience.

unique and forceful æsthetic than can simply be achieved by activating a pull-down menu.

While traditional skills will still be needed, it is the design entrepreneur that will have the best chance of using them to create beautifully-produced and designed products. In the current climate clients are becoming less and less interested in paying for good design. It is only when the designer is determining how the resources will be spent that design will be properly prioritized. Maybe in time we may even be able to shake off the current execrable level of accepted graphic taste from our boots and raise everyone's expectations to demand good design as a matter of course. On a recent trip, I picked up a copy of Steve Martin's novella *Shopgirl* at the airport. This beautifully written, designed and produced little trade paperback (not some extravagantly-priced specialist art publication) was such a pleasure to look at, hold and read, that it restored my faith that one day little gems like this may become the norm rather than the very rare exception. But it may well be that we, the designers, are the ones that will need to be in the driving seat. We have the talent, we have the skills, (maybe we will have to steal the money), what we need now is the will to bury the traditional ways in which we have operated, and to reinvent ourselves and reestablish our professional values.

The designer is dead. Long live the designer. ■

Editor's note: Many of the finest Design Issues essays are available in the book of the same name which has been compiled by DK Holland, the editor of this column, and co-published by Communication Arts *and Allworth Press. To purchase the book, visit* **www.allworth.com.**

Give us your best design on Cougar.

all for entries.

rofessionals: To enter, send a recent design printed on Weyerhaeuser Cougar® Opaque with your name and ddress to the address below. ***Professional entries must be postmarked by 7/31/02.***

tudents: Send a recent piece designed to be printed on uncoated paper with your name, address and school the address below. Student entries must be postmarked by 12/31/02.

ailey & Associates
Veyerhaeuser Cougar Design Contest
687 Melrose Ave.
Vest Hollywood, CA 90069
Categories include: Annual Reports, Brochures, Collateral Material, Calendars, Catalogs, Direct Mail, Posters.
Io to cougaropaque.com for complete rules and details.

FLAT RATE

World class images with licensing legs

Flat Rate licensing is a whole new way to
use top-tier images without the hassle

One flat rate price (small)
One file size (big)
Unlimited use for the designated end user
Only from Comstock.

Making the Visual Verbal

By John Paul Caponigro

"Pictures should be seen and not heard." "If we could communicate what we want to communicate with words, then we'd be writers not artists." The words had rained down on me so many times that my mind had been saturated with the idea. While it reflects some truth, chiefly that a text (written or verbal) can never be a substitute for an image, it can also be misleading. Pictures have always been, continue to be, and will always be talked about—particularly by artists.

Growing up in an artistic family, the parade of visitors and people we visited included many types of artists from musicians to sculptors and most frequently photographers. The topics of conversation were far-reaching and colorful. Often there would be complaints about what had been written about their own work, sometimes about what had been written about each other's work, or what had been written about other artists' work. Then, if they existed, out would come quotes from an artist's personal writings that were used to illuminate, reinforce or refute varied points of view. (Artist's letters, journals, interviews and statements have always held a special position in the history of art. They have forever shaped the commentary that surrounds their work.) Inevitably, the very same artists, who claimed that artists should remain mute, would be lured into giving a lecture or an interview about their work. Artists approach the process of making the visual verbal with mixed feelings; part trepidation, part confirmation, part validation. To be sure, while there are many pitfalls to be avoided, there are many positive byproducts to making the visual verbal.

Writing can illuminate new avenues of inquiry for the viewer and in so doing enrich the entire viewing process, including the subsequent viewing process of future works by other artists. Writing is a process of revelation. It is a process of making thought visible. It is a matter of clarifying a process of thinking. By making what was intuitively sensed visible to the conscious mind, the familiar is clarified and the unfamiliar is brought to light.

Writing about images is inevitable. This kind of writing has always been there. It always will be. Someone, somewhere, sometime will write about your images. You have a great deal to contribute to the process. Along the way, you're likely to find that writing about your work will be extremely revealing.

Many positive things happen when you engage writing. You will understand your work better. You will be able to communicate more clearly about your work. You will affirm the strengths of your work. You will be able to chart your own artistic development over time. You may even be able to uncover the seeds that will provide future growth in your work.

There are a variety of ways to make the visual verbal. There are artist's journals, artist's statements and writing exercises that can be used to get to the core of the inner life of work. There are ways to prepare for interviews; these days many interviews are conducted through writing over the Internet. There are lectures, and writing and rehearsing creates a solid structure for them. Writing can be a tremendous aid to any creative endeavor at any stage in the process.

Distilling

Certain kinds of writing exercises can get the creative juices flowing. Whenever I want to understand an image, a series or a body of work better, I try word association. Association

I want
air

I need
gettyimages.com

can work in several ways. You can cluster words and phrases around an image drawing widely from any association that might spring to mind in a linear fashion (Freud's method) or stay closer to the subject at hand returning to the same source before each new word or phrase is generated (Jung's method). Do both and note the difference. Here's the key; don't censor yourself. No matter how absurd, write all your responses down. You'll have conventional responses, rhyme, make links to current events, even rethink other people's thoughts, but amid all of the machinations of the everyday mind, information from your subconscious will well up if you approach it with an open and non-judgmental frame of mind. This is where pure gold is found. You'll quickly discover connections and feelings you hadn't consciously recognized. Next, you'll want to distill the pool of material these associations generate, focusing on the responses that seem most relevant or significant. Edit them down to the essentials. Then prioritize them. Going further, you can extract themes by making connections between related material. These can form a framework for current comment and future work.

Another very useful technique is amplification. Once you know the qualities or themes that lie within your work, elaborate them. Find all the other ways to say the same things. Say more. You may find the material you're missing is lying in wait for you. One very useful technique is to give voice to a work or the elements within a work. If they could tell you their story, what would they say? These kinds of exercises develop a new level of intimacy with your work. You'll understand it on levels that you might not have imagined before.

I hadn't realized the parallels and connections between two bodies of my own work until I compared the associations and distillations I had done for each separately. Though the work looked different and the subject was quite different (nude and landscape), fully a third of the words and phrases were the same. Despite their differences, at heart their themes were the same. In the long run, this was my own theme. I ended up understanding individual images, both bodies of work, the entire course of my work to date, and myself better. This allowed me to focus and develop that even further.

Journaling

While the personal writings of many famous artists have later been made public, most journals are highly personal and their contents were never intended to be shared. Your journals need only be seen by and be influential to you. A journal is a safe haven for you to explore. Much more than making a permanent record, a touchstone to return to in future years, an artist's journal serves the purpose of exploration. The process of reflection is always a process of revelation.

There are many kinds of journals: chronicles of inspiration, acknowledgements of influence, charts of personal progress including milestones, dream books, hopes for the future, letters to a past self, letters to a confidant. (There have been great correspondences throughout the history of art.) There are even visual journals containing personal sketches, clippings of influential images by other artists, or reproductions of sympathetic work recently found. You can be as creative with your journals as you are with your images. You might even have several, each with a purpose all its own.

Writing is a process of revelation. It is a process of making thought visible. It is a matter of clarifying a process of thinking. By making what was intuitively sensed visible to the conscious mind, the familiar is clarified and the unfamiliar is brought to light.

While you never know which details will be the most significant in the future, many journals often contain too much detail. A list of minute details and trivia make it hard to get to what's important. You may find an emotional, psychological or philosophical history to be more valuable. If a journal doesn't help you find clarity, if it doesn't reinvigorate your personal inquiry, if the process of creating it doesn't ultimately change the way you see, then it's of limited use. What should be included above all are the things that change the way you see and in the process who you are and will become. A history of passion is much more useful than a history of dry facts. While one might serve as fuel for a future fire, only one can strike a spark.

If you find that you are disappointed that you haven't kept a journal, or a particular kind of journal, it's never too late to start. And, you can write "backwards." Journal entries that look back on the significant events in your life can often be the most rewarding. What's more, the treasures that are unearthed along the way are often the most valuable and they are certainly the most relevant at the time you reclaim them.

I have many kinds of journals. While it's a good idea to take

SIS has 4,140 illustrations of "business."
Most stock agencies don't have that many <u>illustrations</u>.

some care with the container for your journals, I find I prefer loose leaf sheets of paper that I later collect into folders. I sort them by content; one for dreams, one for ideas, one for sketches off the top of my head, one for sketches from materials I have collected, one for significant influences over time (I've written backwards to age one), one for reproductions of images I appreciate, one for images I find influential, one for major events throughout a year, one for particular insights over the years. Any one of these themes is simply a useful container to focus a thought process.

Artist's statements

While a journal is a private matter, an artist's statement is meant to be made public. Like a journal, an artist's statement can be approached in many ways and serves many functions. An artist's statement can be used to clarify a thought process, to introduce a body of work to viewers, provide useful excerpts for another's writing, create the foundation for a lecture, or set the stage for an interview. If you haven't written an artist's statement, do. Use this mantra as a starting point; one word, one phrase, one sentence, one paragraph, one page.

Robb Carr, a good friend of mine, quietly caught me off guard one night, "If you could sum up your work in one sentence, what would that be?" I was at a loss for words. How can you reduce a life's work to a few words? I realized that I had been asked a profound question. I returned to my room that night and there on my bedside table was my answer in two words; I was reading Chet Raymo's *Natural Prayers*. I had written several artist's statements, still I was unprepared for a very simple and useful question. Now I upped the ante. Could I do it in one word? Using spare moments collected throughout a few days I had my answers. (Reflections—Natural prayers—My work is about the perception of nature and the nature of perception. You'll find several artist's statements on my Web site **www.johnpaul caponigro.com**)

How frequently should an artist's statement be done? It should be done after the creation of a new body of work, perhaps to understand a single image, to understand a series of images, or to articulate a personal philosophy. Do not wait to be called to write, plan to write.

I strongly recommend writing artist's statements after work has been generated. If a statement is written beforehand, it can guide your efforts too strongly. Then exploration is limited and the surprises contained in the work itself, the ones that bring about the greatest personal transformation and growth, may not arise. Every process has a wisdom all its own that can only be revealed by submitting to it. This is true of writing.

One form of statement is essential for any endeavor—a mission statement. If you think that only traditional businesses need them, think again. Plan for the future. Shape your destiny rather than being shaped by circumstance and happenstance. Set reasonable goals for one, two, three, five and ten years. Revisit them frequently; revise them annually.

Having set goals based on the accomplishments of each previous year, I've exceeded them each year for the last ten years. I wouldn't have been able to do that if I hadn't taken the time to focus and organize my thoughts in writing. Doing this work generates real, tangible benefits.

A history of passion is much more useful than a history of dry facts. While one might serve as fuel for a future fire, only one can strike a spark.

Lectures

At some point in time, it is likely that you will be called upon to make a public presentation about your work. It's not likely that you'll want to write out a lecture word for word. Outlines are generally best. They structure the course of a presentation. They often contain markers for introductions, key transitions and conclusions. An outline is a good thing to review shortly before giving the presentation and to have on hand during the presentation to keep you on track.

If you think of ways to make a presentation better, before, during or after, write them down. There's always room for improvement and the challenge will keep you on your toes. If you make a presentation different each time, even if it's just slightly different, it will always seem fresh.

While you don't want to cite too many references, citing a few is good form. They can lend validation and credibility to almost any presentation. You may want to collect relevant quotes and readings from significant historical sources. Whenever I read, I'm constantly on the lookout for this kind of material. I mark the pages that contain anything I think might be useful, now or in the future. By the same token it can be useful to cite a few influences. Citing your appreciation of similar works by other artists and any parallels that exist often helps an audience feel more at ease with new work.

I find it useful to have several kinds of lectures at hand; chronological, thematic, technical.

Public speaking is difficult at first, but it gets easier with practice. I used to marvel at people who could get up in front of a crowded auditorium and deliver a presentation of any kind. Now I feel comfortable talking to crowds of people, often to several hundred people at a time, and I do so routinely. Getting there took preparation and practice. Now my goal is to do it better each time. I actually look forward to the challenge.

Interviews

Interviews take place in a variety of media—e-mail, phone, radio and television. Each medium has its own strengths. Plan to play to those. Regardless of which medium the interview takes place in, start with an agenda. You might write that agenda in bullet point form. Then flesh out the points with succinct statements.

Interviews via e-mail are written; you have ample time to consider your word choice and can often make longer, more complex statements that can be tightly orchestrated. The downside is that a written interview can become stiff. Stay loose. Remember to keep things fresh and spontaneous.

Interviews by phone and radio are very similar to one another. The major difference is that at a radio station you usually have a physical presence as well as a voice to interact with. But, remember, the listener only hears voices. Project, don't go too fast, speak in full sentences, don't repeat phrases too often, and eliminate the word "um" from your vocabulary. Come with several short statements prepared and rehearsed. Ask yourself the questions you'd like to be asked and the ones you think you might be asked and answer them. Whenever possible, share the list of questions and answers with the interviewer. Quite often they appreciate your help. Even if they or you don't use the exact words you prepared, your answers will show that you were prepared.

Interviews on television are perhaps the most challenging. Time is short. You need to react to the questions put to you and communicate what you want to say in a short amount of time. Write several succinct statements (soundbites) and memorize them. You can't read your lines onscreen. Then tailor your performance to the moment. You'll have to improvise, but if you come in with a few riffs at your fingertips you'll be ready to deliver the best performance possible. Television is performance under pressure. You can reduce the pressure by being prepared ahead of time. Use the remaining pressure for adrenaline. Have fun with it and your performance will be animated and memorable.

While you don't want them to be the sum of your statements, personal anecdotes are very useful. They humanize any statement and allow people to empathize with you. Anecdotes that share something you have in common with your audience are particularly effective.

Finally, always make or get a copy of anything that is published in any media on your work. You can use it for future promotional efforts. You are your greatest archive.

For the past decade, I've had the privilege of interviewing many of my colleagues. I've always approached this work as if I were the artist's ally. Comparing notes with other writers, watching how they approach an interview, listening to the reactions of artists to the interviews they've given, being interviewed myself, I've seen things from many perspectives. It's helped me to understand the interview process better, both its limitations and what it can be in the best of situations. I recommend you practice. Try interviewing yourself. Then get a friend or colleague to interview you. If you do, you'll not only be better prepared for interviews with new acquaintances, you'll learn many things along the way.

Write, write, write or Just Do It

Many people who do not consider themselves writers are intimidated by the thought of writing. But all will admit that writing serves many functions and there are many kinds of writing and writers. Everyone can write. Not all significant writing is great literature. It doesn't have to be. Your writing need only be significant. Ultimately it's what you have to say that's most important, not how you say it. In her book *One Continuous Mistake*, Gail Sher offers four noble truths for writers: "Writers write. Writing is a process. You don't know what your writing will be until the end of the process. If writing is your practice, the only way to fail is not to write." The same could be said of any artistic process. It could also be said that all artists can benefit from writing. After you create, use writing to deepen your understanding of the product you've created and the process you've gone through. You will be richly rewarded for your efforts. ∎

© 2002 John Paul Caponigro

Editor's note: John Paul's advice goes way beyond the practical. It is also a supportive reminder that we have work that should be known, talked about and understood, not only by ourselves, but by ever-expanding audiences.

—Wendy Richmond

POSSIBLE CLIENTS FOR STOCK IMAGE
#SHNA-00149:

①

Real Estate Broker

②

Children's Book Publisher

③

Exorcist

WORKBOOK**stock.com**

We provide extraordinary images.
The rest is up to you.

Why Should Anyone Hire You?

BY BARBARA GORDON

If major corporations ran their advertising and marketing the way some freelancers do, they wouldn't be in business. No matter what is going on in our industry, no matter how bad the business cycle, there is always work to be had and someone is getting that work. The axiom of "Nothing happens until a sale is made" is always true in business.

What got me thinking about the poor marketing and promotion of many freelancers stems from what I have been experiencing in my own business. Freelancers contact me all the time looking for a representative. Usually they send me a postcard with their Web site on it, or a résumé telling me how well they did in school or at former positions they held—and how much they need a job or work. While all of this is necessary, there is little to indicate why I should represent them, very little motivation to drop my selling efforts on behalf of the people I already represent and spend hours looking at Web sites.

When I mentioned this to a creative director friend of mine, he agreed with me and said that he too didn't have the time to pursue anonymous inquiries from freelancers. His sentiments were further echoed by many other art buyers that I spoke with. I decided this is a subject that freelancers must address.

When a corporation sells you something, they conduct focus groups and market surveys to determine: 1. Is there a market for this product? 2. What or who is the market for this product? 3. How do I reach that market? (Politicians also do this to get elected and reelected.) While I'm not suggesting that every freelancer has the funds to set up focus groups or do marketing surveys, freelancers have got to give prospective clients a reason to buy what they are selling.

Advertising, Web sites, competitions and publicity are still a must, but when making a direct approach to a client—and ideally every approach should be direct—you must give the buyer a reason for hiring you over the competition.

For example, in addition to the work, list some of the talents or attributes you can bring to the job: I'm good at concepting, character development, product development, location finding, research, saving money, meeting tight deadlines, available on a 24-hour basis. You fill in the blanks. Without getting too wordy, give a few examples of your accomplishments, i.e., "The character I developed to promote ABC helped increase sales by 40%."

Another point, I *always* stop to read the letters and look at the work of freelancers who are aware of who I represent and the kinds of work I do. The inquiries that come on a postcard with a Web site listed and the phrase, "Need a rep" are less compelling. To carry this analogy a little further, how would you feel about a company that only sent you a postcard that read, "Buy my cereal, car, candy, makeup, beverage?" That's why, through advertising and marketing we are told how a particular product or service will make us richer, safer, happier, healthier, more attractive to the opposite sex. (I don't know if we can convince our prospective clients of all that, but you get the idea.)

So how does the freelancer do this without focus groups and market surveys? We're not in this creative business for nothing. Freelancers need to look objectively at what they have to offer and brutally analyze what they have to sell.

Why should anyone hire you over your competitors? Often,

Sally Wern Comport   Hala Wittwer   Patrick Faricy   Michael Koelsch

Mark Elliott   James Bernardin   Cliff Nielsen   Robert Neubecker

Guy Francis   Ronnie Lawlor   Brett Helquist   Greg Swearingen

Amy Bates   Mike Dietz   Gris Grimly   Glin Dibley

NY 212-333-2551
LA 323-874-5700
www.shannonassociates.com

Representing over 100 artists
in traditional, digital, and
multi-media

SHANNON

it helps to get a few people together to honestly examine each others' strengths and weaknesses. It is generally easier for another pair of eyes to see the real strength and weaknesses in another's work. As a rep, I am often surprised to see something that's obviously commercial, or a market that a freelancer should go after, that the freelancer is blind to.

Take time, quiet time, to really analyze your work, habits and get a real evaluation of your selling strengths. This may take weeks, but it can be one of the most valuable uses of your time. A business has to evaluate its inventory for what it has to sell and how to sell it. Ask family, friends, children (young children especially), "What do you see in my work? What do you like or don't like? What would my work be good for (product-wise)?"

Once you get some ideas about your salient points, try them out on your Web site, direct mail or an ad. See what reactions you get. When you get an assignment, ask the person why you were picked, file the info in your marketing inventory. It often helps to analyze other freelancers' work and approaches. I am amazed at the non-artistic approaches another freelancer will take to get a big assignment or receive major publicity, and once I dissect it, find that sometimes I can use a variation on that theme for someone I represent. This is what focus groups and market surveys are all about, people discussing what makes them want to buy and what makes them react to one product over another.

We're all aware of the changes that are taking place in our industry today, especially those surrounding the protection of our creative rights, and we must all get involved in this battle. But while the struggle is going on, you must continue to sell and promote your product. Keep using your selling and marketing points to get the work and recognition you deserve.

Technology has changed and is still changing our world, but the adage still holds "Nothing happens until the sale is made." What do you have to sell? Why should anyone hire you? Learn that and succeed. ■

freelance

Pictures you NEED and pictures you've dreamed about

The Personal Picture Vault:

Outstanding customer service!

Great Website Features.

Photography, Illustration, Backgrounds, Photo-Objects, Photo-Illustrations, Abstractions

your online Personal storage system.

Unique royalty-free images

brandXpictures™

1.866.427.2639   www.brandXpictures.com

EYE-PC

There's a Xerox network printer tha[
the page at a stunning 22 ppm

With Xerox color, details pop and get noticed. The Xerox Phaser® 7700 tabloid color laser printer will surprise you in countless ways. It not only prints 22 ppm, color or black & white, but speeds out your first color page in just 13 seconds. prints up to 11 x 17 full-bleed, with 1200 dpi for the photograph color quality you and your clients demand. And PhaserMatch

PPING

elivers vivid color that leaps off
here's a new way to look at it.

lor management software ensures the colors you
ant are what you get. It's just what you'd expect
om one of the full line of Xerox network printers.

To see what a difference detailed color can make,
simply give us a call at 1-877-362-6567 ext. 1872
or visit us at **xerox.com/officeprinting/frog1872**

Xerox Phaser 7700
$6,999*

E-Right Triumphs for Creators

By Tad Crawford

Creators have triumphed in important federal court decisions clarifying the ownership of electronic rights. In *Tasini* v. *the New York Times, Inc.*, the United States Supreme Court ruled that creators who had contributed to magazines had not given permission for their articles to be incorporated into online electronic databases. This confirmed the rationale of an important case involving photography, *Greenberg* v. *National Geographic*, in which a CD-ROM created by *National Geographic* of all of its back issues was found to violate the rights of photographers whose images had been published in the magazine.

The *Tasini* case

Jonathan Tasini is president of the National Creators Union and a strong advocate for authors' rights. When he received a payment for an article for *New York Newsday*, he found language on the back of the check indicating that if he signed and cashed the check he would be giving up his electronic rights. While the best course of action might have been to send the check back and ask for a new check without anything written on the reverse, instead Tasini boldly crossed out the language and cashed the check. When he learned that *Newsday* had licensed electronic rights for his article to the Nexis online database, he joined with five other creators who had similar experiences to sue some of the nation's most prominent newspapers, magazines and online information providers.

In federal district court in Manhattan, the judge disappointed the creators. Although the judge determined that the creators had not signed any contracts that would be sufficient to transfer electronic rights, the judge believed that the case turned on "whether the electronic defendants produced 'revisions,' authorized under Section 201(c) of the Copyright Act, of the publisher defendants' collective works." A collective work is one composed of many separate parts, such as a magazine. Without a written agreement specifying which rights are transferred, the publisher of a collective work is presumed under the copyright law to obtain the right to publish the contribution (such as an article) in the collective work, to publish the contribution in any future edition of the collective work, and to publish the contribution in any future revision of the collective work. Finding the question to be of first impression, the court ultimately decided that the disputed electronic reproductions were, in legal terms, revisions of defendants' collective triworks and observed that,

"plaintiffs' real complaint lies in the fact that modern technology has created a situation in which revision rights are much more valuable than anticipated as of the time that the specific terms of the Copyright Act were being negotiated."

Appealing the *Tasini* decision

Unwilling to accept defeat, Tasini and his co-plaintiffs appealed to the Second Circuit Court of Appeals. To the delight of creators, the appellate court viewed that matter quite differently from the district court. The Second Circuit's opinion noted, "There is no feature peculiar to the databases at issue in this appeal that would cause us to view them as 'revision.'" The court pointed out that Nexis, for example, contains thousands or millions of individually retrievable articles, so it can hardly be considered a revision of a collective work such as a magazine or newspaper.

The defendants then appealed to the United States Supreme Court which, in the middle of 2001, handed down a historic decision affirming the Second Circuit. By a 7–2 vote the Supreme Court found in favor of the creators, agreeing that "The Databases offer users individual articles, not intact periodicals." Thus, the databases could not be revisions of periodicals. The Supreme Court sent the case back to the District Court to determine what remedies, including damages, should be awarded to creators.

Greenberg v. *National Geographic*

The *Greenberg* case revolved around the same issue as the *Tasini* case, except that photographs rather than articles had been contributed to *National Geographic*. Jerry Greenberg had done four assignments for *National Geographic* and either had rights in his photographs reassigned to him by *National Geographic* or provided by contract that the rights would terminate 60 days after publication in the magazine. As the Court of Appeals pointed out, the CD-ROM created by *National Geographic* in 1996 to collect every issue of the magazine since 1888 used Greenberg's images in three ways: (1) one 25-second animation of 10 different covers included a cover with a diver photographed by Greenberg; (2) all the covers and interiors of the magazines were scanned and included on the CD-ROM; and (3) a search feature allowing viewers to navigate through the CD-ROM (and thus find Greenberg's images).

The court posited that an evaluation of Greenberg's claims turned on the interpretation of Section 201(c) of the copyright law, the same section involved in the *Tasini* case. After reviewing the competing arguments, the court concluded: "However, common-sense copyright analysis compels the conclusion that the Society…has created a new product… in a new medium, for a new market that far transcends any privilege of revision or other mere reproduction envisioned in Section 201(c)." In addition, the court found that the use of the diver cover in the animated sequence violated Greenberg's right to make or control the making of derivative works (i.e., works derived from an original but then transformed, such as a movie made from a novel).

More recently, a number of other photographers have come forward to sue *National Geographic* on the same grounds. As many as a dozen photographers, including Pete Turner, Jay Maisel and Peter Menzel, are seeking to bring a class action and alleging damages of $100 million or more.

A Rosetta Stone?

In the book publishing world, the important case of *Random House* v. *Rosetta Books* revolved around contractual interpretation. From the 1960s into the 1980s, a number of prominent authors, including Kurt Vonnegut, William Styron and Robert B. Parker, had published their books with Random House pursuant to a contract granting Random House the right to "print, publish and sell the work[s] in book form." When these authors entered into contracts for e-books with Rosetta Books, Random House brought an action for copyright infringement and asked for an injunction to stop Rosetta Books from selling the e-book versions.

Since many publishers had contracts similar to that used by Random House, the decision promised to have a huge impact on whether creators would control and financially benefit from the exploitation of electronic rights in their books. Denying Random House's request for an injunction, the court ruled that Random House is "not likely to succeed on the merits of its copyright infringement claim." Random House appealed, but the Court of Appeals affirmed the decision of the lower court in favor of Rosetta Books. The case may go to a full trial, but Random House would appear to have little hope of winning after this initial decision.

A warning for creators

These three cases are great victories for creators in the important area of e-rights. Based on these decisions, creators who do not explicitly sign away e-rights in a written contract are likely to have retained such rights. The danger now is that publishers will attempt to exert their often superior bargaining strength to force creators to grant e-rights. In a sense, the conflict over e-rights is a reflection of the earlier battle over work-for-hire contracts, which not only gave all rights to the publisher but also made the publisher the "creator" of the work. Creators' organizations strove to educate writers and artists about the dangers of work-for-hire contracts. Now that the publishers have learned they can't grab electronic rights on the basis of far-flung legal interpretations, creators have to fear—and expect—that publishers will be offering one-sided contracts that seek to gain electronic rights.

What should creators do to combat this? Every creator should be prepared to negotiate the contracts offered to him or her. A clear distinction should be made between rights in physical media, such as printed books or magazines, and rights in electronic media (such as Web site usage or e-books). A creator should only license traditional rights and electronic rights if adequate and separate remuneration will be paid. If this is not the case, the creator should carefully reserve electronic rights (if traditional rights are being licensed) and traditional rights (if electronic rights are being transferred).

For *Business and Legal Forms for Graphic Designers*, *Business and Legal Forms for Photographers*, and *Business and Legal Forms for Illustrators*, I developed the following contractual language to protect the creator who is only transferring traditional rights, "All rights not expressly granted hereunder are reserved to the Creator, including but not limited to all rights in preliminary materials and all electronic rights. For purposes of this agreement, electronic rights are defined as rights in the digitized form of works that can be encoded, stored, and retrieved from such media as computer disks, CD-ROM, computer databases, and network servers." If creators insist on written contracts with such protective language, their ownership of electronic rights may become a valuable source of future income. ∎

Have Heroes

BY LUKE SULLIVAN

When I first got into this business back in 1978, I had heroes. In fact, I had a list of heroes. Their names were all written in the indexes of the 1977 and '78 One Show annuals. I saw these people as gods. I studied every one of their ads. I memorized their copy. And I dreamed that one day I'd see my name on the list next to theirs.

Having heroes is good. Having them the way I did, wasn't.

Having heroes the way I did probably kept me from doing better work in my early years. Because when you deify these ordinary people the way I did, you preclude the possibility of ever doing anything as well as they do. They're gods—you're just a guy. In an apartment.

With pimples.

There's no way, I thought, I'll ever be that good. So the idea of ever doing it as well as they remained only a wild hope, something years in the future perhaps, but certainly beyond the horizon.

My sycophancy also made me do stupid things.

Try this on.

In 1983, I was in New York City interviewing at some big agencies, one of which was the famous shop, Scali McCabe Sloves. After my interview with the great art director, Lars Anderson (remember the Maxell ad with the guy being blown back into his seat?), I was boarding the elevator back down to Third Avenue when who should also get on but Sam Scali himself—one of my heroes.

This was only my second trip to New York and so, like a nerd, I had a Polaroid camera. I mean, I had one right there with me.

Without thinking, I said: "Mind if I take our picture, Mr. Scali?"

Holding the camera backwards at arm's length, I blinded both myself and the famous art director with a cheap flash bulb. As the dazed and, I'm sure, irritated man disappeared into the New York crowd, I figured I had scored The Big One. (Yes, that's it! I'll use this picture in a cool follow-up letter to Mr. Scali!) A very bad idea, I'm sorry to say, I immediately followed up on.

I must have had some sense of how much I'd invaded his personal space because a line from the follow-up letter I mailed went something like: "Even if I don't get the job now, should I do well in the shows this year, I hope you'll at least remember me as 'that idiot in The One Show' and not just as 'that idiot in the elevator'." Even now, I shudder to remember this and send my belated apologies to Mr. Scali.

Such goggle-eyed admiration also blinded me to the faults of my heroes. I learned some bad habits from one or two of them, habits I had to break later. Because no matter how cool your hero's ads are, no matter how many One Show medals are on your hero's shelf, he or she's still just a knuckle-head who flosses and twangs stuff on the mirror same as you and me, Jack.

This fact came fully home to me one year when I judged The One Show on a beautiful island in the Caribbean. One of my all-time heroes was also invited to be a judge. I was hoping that, as a judge myself, I might be able to sidel up to him, trade jokes, break bread, do something, anything with The Man.

But an hour into the weekend I realized how little I wanted to be around him. Narcissism poured off my icon like cool air onto your feet in front of an open meat locker.

photonica.com

keyword: summer
search

■ Title: Woman with Hula Hoop
Image #: 3003-011553
Catalog ref: 59-80-1
Photographer: Johner

Search Keyword:
Adults, Caucasians, Clouds,
Dancing, Faces, Females,
Freedom, Full length, Fun,
Grasses, Health, Hula hoops,
Meadows, Motion, One person,
Outdoors, Skies, Summer,
Trees, Women

On the last night when all the judges went out to dinner, I finally laid to rest my idolization. There he was across the restaurant, spit-fire drunk and badgering the local stray dog; yelling at the frightened animal, poking at it and trying to get the rest of us to join him. My hero was a drunk and a schmuck to boot.

There was this other guy I knew once. Killer writer. If you saw him in the award books, you'd go, Whoa, this guy's great! But if you saw him in the agency hallways, you went the other way. Because he was an insufferable, arrogant bore. Everybody in the agency hated him and although we tried to be philosophical about his character, the best we ever came up with was: "Well, if you cut him open, you'd find a heart of gold. And if you didn't, well, hey, you've cut him open!"

I still have heroes. But I admire them now with my former adoration in reins and a modest amount of esteem for my own abilities. Unclouded by envy, I now try to look only at their work and to learn from it.

My heroes change weekly now. This week, it's a young writer at Fallon, Tom Rosen, who just did this great ad for BMW. The ad's on my wall right now; it's the thing to beat. It inspires me.

That's what heroes are good for: to inspire, to teach.

Take them where you find them. They're all over the place. Your career will present you with many heroes to learn from and it will pay to learn how to spot them.

But do your heroes always have to be based on how well they write or art direct? How about how they treat people?

Tom McElligott, my first hero, helped me break into the business. Here he was, the hottest copywriter in all of America, and he took the time to look through my pathetic book, past my bad haircut, and see me as the unformed but passable lump of clay I was. I have been returning the favor ever since, to young people who sit now in my office, over-explaining their books.

Another one of my heroes is my old boss, Mike Hughes, creative director and president of The Martin Agency. (I suppose Mike would prefer to be my hero by dint of his writing prowess.) Well, he is a great writer, but he's on my list today for being a kind and gentle person in a tough, cynical business. I still remember my first interview with him back in 1980-something. He lovingly took a picture of his youngest son

out of his wallet and said, "Children are a constant reminder that there's a life outside of advertising." I have remembered that advice to this day.

Don Just, now of Work (also in Richmond) was the first account guy I ever saw stand up and cheer upon being shown a great creative solution. You cannot imagine the power that kind of reaction has on the creative soul. I would have walked over coals to solve Don's problems. I hope my own staff would do the same for me today.

The last hero (on today's list anyway) is my old friend and colleague, Bob Barrie; possibly the world's greatest art director, certainly the world's most decorated one. From Bob, I

No matter how cool your hero's ads are, no matter how many One Show medals are on your hero's shelf, he or she's still just a knucklehead who flosses and twangs stuff on the mirror same as you and me, Jack.

learned many things. One of which was how not to suck. But more important, Bob taught me about the lasting power of resiliency. A client could keep killing his ideas and Bob would always come back with more. He's a sort of *Halloween*, Michael-Meyers of Concepts. There is no stopping him. And he never whined. In all the time I worked with him, Bob never whined. Ever.

The fact that Bob was winning One Show pencils in 1982 and is still winning them today seems testimony to the lasting power of resiliency. (It also helps not to suck.)

So, yes, have heroes. Aspire. Want to be better than you are.

But temper your discontent.

Remember, there was a time when even your heroes were quite awful and stayed very late at the agency laying out ads that truthfully and sincerely blew. Remember, even your heroes still have their bad days and don't always do great work on the first few tries. Remember, heroes can be idolized for many talents, not just for writing and art directing. And that being great on paper is never as important as actually being a great person. ∎

Looking for the perfect designer?

Aquent Online Portfolios

Thousands of our employees' portfolio pieces are now online, so it's even easier to find the perfect designer. Search under 38 design specialties, by keyword and location. Instantly see thumbnails, descriptions, and résumés. And rest assured, we've met and qualified every designer in person.

So, the next time you need just the right freelancer, contractor, or permanent hire, go to aquent.com. Or call us at 877-2-AQUENT, and our agents will find the perfect designer for you.

AQUENT

American Institute of
Graphic Arts

Adobe

lynda.com

National Association of
Photoshop Professionals

Association of
Internet Professionals

Art Directors
Club

Trillium Press

The land of yes offers new ideas for illustrators

By Ruth Hagopian

In the middle of the night, when thoughts of art and commerce interrupt his sleep, Trillium Press president Richard Lang passes the time by memorizing poetry. He recalled lines from poet Wallace Stevens:

"It was not from the vast ventriloquism,
of sleep's faded papier-mâché...

It was like a new knowledge of reality."

The words speak directly to the atmosphere Lang and founder/director David Salgado have cultivated at Trillium Press, a fine art print studio in Brisbane, California. Based in an industrial park bordering a lagoon ten minutes south of San Francisco, the heart of the studio lies in collaborating with 'maker people,' who want to create art while breaking through boundaries of tradition and technique.

Illustrator Mark Ulriksen began making prints when buyers wanted copies of his published work. His colorful figures of people and dogs are printed one and two at a time on the

Iris printer. "I took out an ad in *Bark* magazine," he said. "I have to find ways to get it out there. When someone sees my work, I can now make it available."

"Now we're working with illustrators who are actually marketing their illustrations as art work, which is what it should be," Lang said.

"If he was doing lithography, it could cost more than ten thousand dollars. The startup cost for Iris prints is between four and five hundred dollars."

Traditional printing techniques have long been established at Trillium Press by master printer Salgado. Silk-screen, monotype, lithography, intaglio and photogravure printing are available to artists as well as giclée, or Iris digital prints.

What they really like to do is mix it up, experiment and explore the possibilities of 'vertical integration,' their term for combining different printing techniques in a single work. "Normally various media rarely or never, mix," Salgado said. "Our approach is to bring it in rather than push it away."

A successful alliance between illustrator Jed Morfit and Noah Lang, Trillium's partner and technical expert in digital media, resulted in two projects for Morfit. A series of nine illustrations on a grid were printed and compositionally changed for each final print. He also printed individual drawings that were sold at Open Studios, a citywide art exhibition in San Francisco.

"It opens up a lot of possibilities," Morfit said. "I used to use them as portfolio pieces, but they're too expensive to send to art directors who get coffee stains on them or don't send them back. If someone is interested in my work, I can bring them to my studio and say, 'This is what I can show to you.'" Morfit sells the individual prints for $150 a piece.

J. Otto Siebold also worked with Noah Lang on a combination of giclées and monotypes that were then hand-painted and collaged. Siebold spent a week at the print shop with his family and their three dogs. "I broke away from monotype and did things I don't usually do," Siebold said.

Joining ranks with international artists William Wiley, Wayne Thiebaud and Enrique Chagoya, are first-time printmakers and students working at the Trillium studio. A grants program was recently established to subsidize the eight thousand dollar weekly cost to work there.

"Usually, all this stuff is available to artists like Frank Stella

YOU CAN GET THERE FROM HERE.

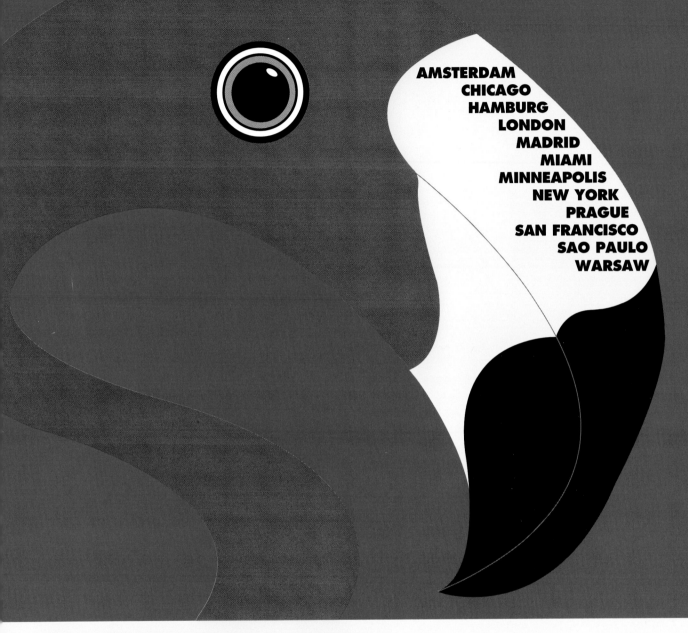

AMSTERDAM
CHICAGO
HAMBURG
LONDON
MADRID
MIAMI
MINNEAPOLIS
NEW YORK
PRAGUE
SAN FRANCISCO
SAO PAULO
WARSAW

After spending a year learning the basics in one of our full time schools in Miami, Minneapolis, San Francisco, Warsaw or São Paulo, students like Reyn spend the next year studying and interning in up to four other cities.

"Finally got that ALL ideas are cool. Be open and ideas can go far. Thanks to Dave and Pete from TBWA. And, oh yeah, pollution sucks."

"Kissed a girl with B.O. Seemed like the European thing to do. I don't know who said this, but here's a quote, 'The harder I work, the luckier I get.' Got to work at Jung von Matt, one of the trippiest agencies on the planet."

"Jung von Matt liked me so much they didn't let me leave. Now I work on cool stuff like BMW and great local clients like Sparkasse and Cinemaxx."

5th Quarter: Minneapolis   7th Quarter: Amsterdam

6th Quarter: London   8th Quarter: Hamburg

"My hardest quarter. I learned I was stupid. But my teachers taught me how to reach people at a high level and do it creatively too. I'm still stupid though."

"My first agency work. It was so much fun I drooled on myself from laughing so hard. They gave us bikes to ride to work. My partner Ben and I started a biking posse and introduced ghost riding to the city. Clients are crazy. Just do what you do."

MIAMI AD SCHOOL'S QUARTER AWAY PROGRAM

For more info visit www.miamiadschool.com or call 800.858.3190.

Mark Ulriksen, *Little Dog*, 2001. Edition of 50, co-published by Trillium Press and the artist. Paper size: 32 × 23, image: 28 × 18½, Iris print.

and James Rosenquist, but why not make it available to an undergraduate print student or anyone who gets it and walks through the door," Richard Lang said. "To offer that to someone with no track record just because you have faith in them, that's where the grants come in."

Grants will allow nine or ten students from local and national art colleges to develop their work. "In most print shops, the model is, if you're working with an artist of lesser stature, you're diminishing the stature of the higher artists you're working with," Lang said. "Our attitude is, if you think that way, you're living in an unreal world based on politics, manipulation and celebrity."

Lang's all-embracing, inclusive spirit compliments Salgado's introspection and intensity, deeply rooted in feelings of community and abundance. Their motto for Trillium Press is 'The Land of Yes,' a place where they work with blue-collar artists and blue-chip artists. "It's one bus, and everyone's on it," Lang said.

Early in his collaboration with Salgado, Lang's background as an artist and teacher led him to create a series of finely rendered bird heads as black-and-white lithographs. "I wanted to do monotype behind them," he said. "And then

I wanted to dress them up in costumes like Egyptian gods or something. David said, 'Let's try it.'

"It set the whole stage for the rest of my life's work. Now I do digital painting and watercolor painting and cut them out and reform them into other things that really speak to that integration of the minds. And that all came out of somebody saying 'yes' to me."

Salgado studied at Tamarind Institute, whose mission in the 1970s was to train American-based master printers to print by hand from stone, a process which dates back to 1797. He opened up his first shop in 1976 and is still on the press 32 years later.

Two of Salgado's printing inventions are unique to the studio. Continuous-tone lithography eliminated the half-tone dot, which is especially significant when an artist prints photographic images combined with hand-drawing and lettering. He also created the right-reading registerable multiple impression monotype which can generate seven to ten identical images from one painting.

"The whole thing about printmaking is the ability to deconstruct," Salgado said. "You have to figure out how to look at

Enrique Chagoya, *The Enlightened Savage*, 2002. Edition of 40, published by Trillium Press. 14 × 16 × 3 over all, digital print of paper and canned food.

something and take it apart into its essential elements and put it back together without losing the life in the process."

At first, Salgado was skeptical about digital printing and incensed when hearing digital technicians with a few years experience being called 'master printers.' "In the beginning, the inks were really horrible and lasted a year to two years," he said. "They were overpriced then, but they worked out the color and every year it got better and better. This is the first valid printmaking media to appear since silk-screen in the 1940s."

Museums and galleries have established collections of giclée prints that were once considered 'unstable.' "The Whitney just bought Chagoya's pieces and The Los Angeles Museum of Contemporary Art has the largest collection of digital printing in the world," Lang said. Collections of digital prints are also found at the Louvre in Paris, London's Tate Gallery and the Toronto Museum, among many others.

Trillium's print and limited-edition book collection is displayed in the gallery area of their 7,000 square foot studio. Their digital room with computers and four Iris printers leads to an adjoining room with lithography, screenprint and monotype presses. The back room is a workshop studio space with moveable walls and a 20 × 20 foot wall space to work on a grand scale.

The idea is to encourage a feeling of intimacy or openness conducive to the artist and their art. "They have to love their own work and they have to be a little scared," Lang said. "They should be counter-phobic—go towards what they're afraid of," he added, pausing to hear part of the long version of "Light My Fire" playing on the studio's newly acquired old record player.

"Collaborating is like having a piece of string on your finger," Salgado said. "You remind the artist that they love their own work and that isn't it great that they can make a living."

Both Salgado and Lang have a no-nonsense approach to the business side of making art. Their first suggestion is to forget the fantasy of instant success after art school. "The myth is that you will graduate from art school, your work will be purchased by the Metropolitan Museum of Art in New York, and you will have arrived," Lang said.

"Like professional basketball players," Salgado added.

"You're in business. You're a manufacturer," Lang said. "Treat it like a business with respect. Don't think that business is bad and don't think you're selling out."

"If you really sell out it means you're committing everything to this," Salgado said. "If you're going to be an artist, be an artist. Then you'll really suffer, but you're going to suffer anyway. As if you could be free from suffering."

Suffering a life in the arts is tempered by the fact that it is also possible to make a living. The variety of ways to sell art is evident in the diversity of artists that come through the Trillium Press doors. Lang and Salgado are encouraged by opportunities that include Web sites, publishers and art fairs.

"This guy comes in. He's a computer programmer," Lang said. "He does wild-ass collages and decides he wants to market them. We suggest he do these little cards. So we print up 1,000 of them and he mailed them out. He's in business now—making more art." ■

Remember Illustration?

By Dugald Stermer

A familiar colloquy: At a party a young woman asked what I "did," meaning, I assumed, for a living. When I answered, "I'm an illustrator," she looked at me blankly for a couple of seconds, then brightened and said, "Children's books." The only noteworthy part about what happened next is that this time it started me thinking. And that, along with the fuss about that odd article about graphic design's purported relationship to illustration in the January/February Design Issues column of this magazine, prompted this article.

First, regarding the aforementioned "Illustration: Graphic Design's Poor Relation," just the title alone should have warned anyone remotely aware of the history and function of illustration that the text that followed would either be misplaced satire, or entirely misinformed; amazingly, it is both. But it served a purpose in that it awakened me, once again, to the misapprehensions many people, some of whom actually practice in the field, have about the art and business of illustration.

Actually, the problem isn't so much one of misunderstanding as it is of no understanding at all. If the interchange outlined in the first paragraph had happened at any time during the first three-quarters of the twentieth century, there would have been no confusion about the job description of illustrator. During that period the nation's mailboxes were full of *Colliers*, *Time*, *The Saturday Evening Post*, *Fortune* and a passel of other magazines sporting illustrated covers, along with many painted advertising and editorial pages inside. And it wasn't all Norman Rockwell Americana either. [Boris] Artzybasheff's frequent cover portraits for *Time* were superbly surreal. Ben Shahn's soulfully spiky paintings and drawings often graced the editorial pages of *Redbook* and *Look*, as well as advertisements for CBS. Richard Gangel, the art director at *Sports Illustrated*, sent Robert Weaver, Tom Allen and others on assignment to illustratively cover major sporting events around the world. *Playboy*, under its art director Art Paul, introduced us to a number of brilliant young illustrators, among them Brad Holland and Kinuko Craft. The late 1950s and '60s saw an explosion of work from Pushpin Studios, to my mind the single most influential phenomenon in graphic design and illustration, worldwide, in the entire twentieth century. (If we were speaking of design alone, then Bauhaus advocates must be allowed their preference.) The work of its partners, Milton Glaser and Seymour Chwast, along with members Jim McMullan, Ed Sorel, Paul Davis and others was extraordinary in its intelligence, wit and craft, but all different in execution and approach. For many young designers and illustrators of those decades, a glance at any new edition of Pushpin's *Graphic* was encouragement to fly. (As an aside, preeminent Cuban graphic artist Alfredo Rostgaard told me he named his dog Milton in honor of, well, you know.)

Illustration? Hell, everyone knew about illustration, from the time Frederic Remington drew the West for *Harper's Review*, to the magical Scribner's Classics illustrated by N.C. Wyeth, through the Gibson Girl and the Arrow Shirt man, through "Uncle Sam Wants You" and "Loose Lips Sink Ships," through Rockwell Kent's stark books and Norman Rockwell's Four Freedoms, and through Coby Whitmore's pretty girls in the *Post* and Vargas's even prettier girls in *Esquire*. The fictional Horatio Hornblower, as illustrated in the *Post*, was as familiar to my parents as Clark Gable. Our image of Santa Claus was essentially formed by Haddon Sundblom's Coca-Cola ads. *Life* magazine, a showcase for photography, was noticeable as an exception. Illustrated

Know.
A thousand times know.

Call for your Free 2002 Salary Guide.

Instant access to salary data that's the most up-to-date in the business can help you attract (and retain)
the best people. It's all here, and it's all free. So it's a know-brainer.
Call today for your copy.

t g THE CREATIVE GROUP®
MARKETING & ADVERTISING PROFESSIONALS

web designers | graphic designers | marketing managers | account managers | copywriters | art directors

888.846.1668 • creativegroup.com

© The Creative Group. EOE

images interpreted, decorated and defined the life of Americans for the better part of the twentieth century.

(On the contrary, no one knew—or, for that matter, knows—what a graphic designer is or does, outside of other graphic designers and their corporate clients, despite the best efforts at self-promotion of what writer and critic Steven Heller has dubbed "the me-too generation" of designers in the 1980s and '90s. Earlier still, back when I practiced in that field, a certain graceful anonymity was a good thing. "The best design never gets noticed," was not a complaint but a credo. Style deferred to content. I know, that seems distantly old school. But building a reputation through informed restraint was a challenge well worth undertaking.)

The matter of why, when and how illustration, as the craft has been practiced, published and understood, has all but disappeared from the public consciousness is a complicated one. That it has become marginalized is even debated, but for the sake of this piece, let's concede that it has. Let's also, temporarily at least, excise easy blame from the equation, as in, "It's all the fault of lazy art directors/visually impaired editors/focus groups/photographers/greedy stock houses/MBAs and lawyers/inferior art schools/lousy illustration/old

illustrators who won't step aside in favor of youth/youth who don't respect their elders/etc." There is likely truth to some of that, but the notion that any faction intentionally set out to shove painted and drawn images to the far reaches of our mass culture is absurd.

I started to re-think this whole dilemma, about a month ago, after spending a quarter century working as an illustrator, and the last several years as a board member of both The [2001] Illustration Conference and The Illustrators' Partnership of America. Before and overlapping all that, I had put in nearly two decades in graphic design and magazine art direction. Back then, I also wrote a pile of articles, reviews and profiles for this very magazine. But I never gave myself sufficient time and distance to try to analyze the vast changes we've recently weathered. It may well be impossible; as the aphorism goes, we don't know who discovered water, but we're pretty sure it wasn't a fish. I'm clearly a fish in this stream; on the other hand, no one but a fish cares. That's one of the symptoms.

Images are everywhere as never before. Drawn, painted, digitized, animated, filmed and photographed—they are ubiquitous. Images are also worth money. They must be because Gates and Getty have invested heavily in hundreds of thousands of them, and they're hardly financial fools. The shame is that generally speaking those pictures are not worth nearly as much to those who made them as they are to those who sell them. And, again in general, fewer original illustrations are being commissioned, and those for lower fees, in some cases much lower, than in the past. They have largely been replaced on the covers and pages of our mass media by photography, much of it indistinguishable from press agent handouts. The few exceptions, like the recent portrait of black CEOs by Dan Adel on the cover of *Newsweek*, seem wistfully nostalgic. The last illustrated cover I remember on *Rolling Stone* was of Bart Simpson, not that they had a choice.

I have a couple of notions about this. Even back in the glorious days of illustration, there was one breed of publication that always sported photographed covers and pages. *Photoplay*, *Modern Screen* and the rest of the fan magazines never commissioned much of anything, but published studio handouts almost exclusively. Perfectly-lit studio mug shots, often hand tinted, were the rule, almost never broken. Who would have guessed that they were the cockroaches of publications, outlasting nearly all other species. Many of the others that survive, do so by adopting their style and lack of substance. Celebrity journalism has infected news magazines, fashion magazines, literary magazines, as well as most shelter, lifestyle and special interest publications. There remains enough demand for brilliant caricatures to keep Al Hershfeld, David

Levine and C.F. Payne, among others, busy; at least I hope they're busy. But studio photography rules, along with the celebrity culture it promotes.

Another thought is that photography, along with generic stock illustration, is relatively risk free. I remember with dismay the recent words of the art director of one of our most respected newspapers, to the effect that they were no longer going to be able to commission illustration because the marketing people had concluded that "illustration disturbs people." This isn't an isolated attitude, but permeates the offices of many formerly inventive publishing institutions. Then too, photography offers a multitude of choices resulting from a single assignment, something many art directors, designers and editors dearly love to tweak over.

Following the trend toward minimizing risk and covering one's backside, there is the well-documented rise in the use of stock illustration, a practice that impoverishes the culture while it enriches the stock houses. I won't belabor the subject, because it would require a whole other article, and because it's too damn depressing. It appears that all American commerce has fallen victim to market researched, focus tested, generic branding. Why should the graphic arts and publishing industries be exceptions?

Some of those few who do continue to commission original illustration are doing so accompanied by startling new contractual demands. We know all too well that page rates haven't increased, dollar for dollar, since about 1910, no exaggeration. But now we have the all-rights contract to contend with. For example, the new contract offered illustrators and photographers by one of the largest media conglomerates in the country states that, upon signing, the artist *relinquishes all rights to the piece in question, the rights to all works commissioned in the past by the publisher, as well as any it might commission in the future, in all existing media and that yet to be invented*. It sounds like a joke, but it's not, as veteran artists' representative Gerry Rapp, the Graphic Artists Guild and The Illustrators' Partnership of America attest. If their struggle to revise those terms is unsuccessful, this model will surely spread. There is profit in grabbing artists' rights, especially if they can be had for free.

Another factor: Much of the function of general interest publications has been usurped by television and the Internet. What our parents and grandparents spent money for at the newsstands and through subscriptions we now receive free, electronically and digitally. And it must be admitted that for the most part, illustrators have been tardy in adapting their work to the new media. Designers are all over the Web, Photoshoping layered Web sites for everyone and anyone. But we still think in terms of the printed page, by

and large, while our public has pretty much found their entertainment and information elsewhere.

There are, indeed, many other factors at work, among the least of which is that a lot of trendy illustration is noticeably free of craft, skill, imagination and intelligence, not to mention communication. It is, in short, not particularly illustrative, just edgy.

The fact remains, at a time when images are everywhere, illustration, as we've known and valued it, seems not obsolete but moribund. And that's curious, because despite the glut of imitative, faddish stuff out there, there are also plenty of skillful, inventive and bright artists either working hard to break through, or laboring even harder to maintain their careers.

Visually interpreting our culture is a marvelous job, a perfect fit for illustrators. But where is it written that we may only initiate work at the behest of art directors and designers, slaves to purchase orders, rights contracts and the printed page? Some excellent artists have already discovered the new animation and illustrated novels (sophisticated comic books) as outlets. Others have started their own publishing companies, while a few have followed the lead of *The Simpsons'* creator Matt Groening and moved to television. The Web, having been found wanting as the world's largest shopping mall, is still an open field for many kinds of communication, including visual storytelling and commentary. In short, there are pictures everywhere; there are just not enough of *our* pictures, published on *our* terms, at least not yet.

I don't have the solutions. I just know we have to begin the search as entrepreneurs, even visionaries, as well as artists, if our art is to survive.

New technologies and media usually defy prognosticators. Recorded music didn't supplant performances or remove pianos and guitars from the home; there are more horses in North America today than there were before automobiles; movies didn't spell the end for the theater, nor did television replace movies, and neither of them spelled doom for the book publishing business as had been widely predicted. The older forms adapted to the changes and survived, even occasionally flourished. There is nothing to suggest that illustration is by definition any more obsolete than the theater, cinema or literature.

What is required, it seems to me, is for us all, veterans and emerging artists alike, together as well as individually, to envision the business of making communicative images as if our entire heritage on the printed page was but a preamble, and not a road map back to a place that no longer exists as we remember it. ■

Design Ranch

Gettin' Some Grit

By Anne Telford

Whoopee Ti-Yi-Yo Git Along Little Dogies…" Heading west from San Antonio, into the famed lush rolling hill country of Texas, you leave the city behind and encounter barbecue joints with their names painted on the roofs, cattle grazing in pastures and Boerne, with its quaint town square with white gazebo, gurgling fountain and all. Evidence of an America that seems to be vanishing. Already the shoulders start to relax from too much time behind a computer.

As soon as you pull into the gate that announces you've arrived at the Guadalupe River Ranch, you know the next couple of days will be completely unlike your normal life.

Driving down the road, the sight of Texas longhorn cattle, emu and sheep, gives more evidence that this will be a different "conference" experience. No big chain hotels with over-air conditioned ballrooms and crystal chandeliers invoking thoughts of *Phantom of the Opera*. No podiums. No PowerPoint presentations. No ponderous design-speak. No thin coffee and semi-stale muffins. This is one place you get to be hands-on, working side-by-side with noted designers, illustrators and photographers. There's art, playtime and naptime (hammocks beckon in the increasingly warm Texas afternoons). If you're doing it right, you can't help getting your hands dirty, and your spirit refreshed. Long views across the rolling green hills, dotted with oak trees, encourage exploration. The Guadalupe River is perfect for tubing. There are horses to ride and a spa where you can receive massage or aromatherapy, if you need a break from artistic endeavors.

April 18–21, around 100 people gathered for the fourth annual Design Ranch, which started off with a welcome from conference founder/master of ceremonies Marc English of Austin-based Marc English Design. Dressed in cowboy regalia, he stood between two monitors showing, what else, but *True Grit*. As John Wayne endured a gun battle, English set the stage for the relaxed proceedings of the next two-and-a-half days. Many in the crowd were repeat attendees. Joel Nakamura, who has attended every year, brought his posse from Santa Fe, and others from Nashville, California, New York and parts between, came for some design R&R. Many sponsors also repeated their

support, and seemed to enjoy the event as much as the attendees. Stephenie Theriot and Tania Gardère-MacLeod from Potlatch; Stora Enso's Patty Jenkins and Brian Woodard; Shirley Richardson of Williamson Printing; Heather Boyd from Fox River Paper and Donna Scoggins of Neenah Paper have been onboard all four years—an impressive record for sponsorship. Mark Fake of Sappi, came back for the second year and Padgett Printing was a new sponsor this year.

A stellar cast of characters—Anita Kunz, Eric Madsen, Steve Sandstrom, James Victore, the Amazing Hancock Brothers, Woody Welch and Judy Schulz—was on hand to teach workshops on everything from illustrated journals and handmade books to stenciled prints, photographs made without cameras or film and 3-D cardboard chairs. Achieving a rare synergy, each workshop seemed to lead effortlessly into the next, in organic fashion so that you could see how different techniques and approaches could influence every aspect of your work.

Steve Sandstrom fashioned innovative color workshops where attendees created their own versions of green, trendy green, orange and trendy orange, then assembled the chips into a personal color fan-guide. The synchronicity in colors between the four workshops was amazing. While we painted, Steve discoursed about color and its application and attendees shared their own reflections on color.

Eric Madsen spoke of drawing on experience to create a visual diary, showing examples from his personal diaries, then provided the tools for attendees to create their first entries and share with others.

Cathie Bleck, absent was represented by due to a sudden death in the family, friends, Austin illustrator Marc Burkhardt and head cowgirl Andrea Bond (Design Ranch chair) who ably stepped in to lead her mask making and marbled paper workshops. (Of course in true fashion, Cathie had sent ahead detailed instructions, while in the midst of everything else.)

James Victore's competitive cardboard workshops produced a variety of chairs sturdy enough to sit on including an electric chair, a toilet and a chair resembling a large bull's head.

focus on an idea
Pete McArthur.com

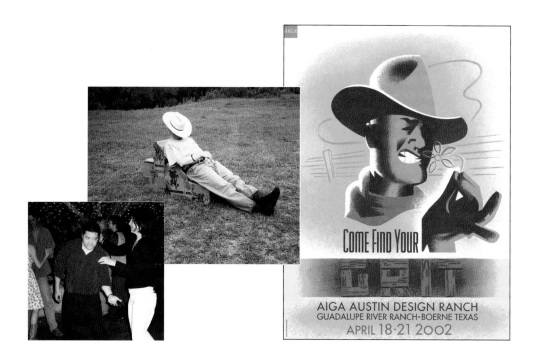

San Francisco Bay Area illustrators Nicholas Wilton and Jennie Oppenheimer painted striking bird portraits of each other in Anita Kunz's anthropomorphic portraits workshops, which produced a variety of amazing works. The workshops ended with a cow patty toss—which allowed Steve Sandstrom to demonstrate his impressive throwing arm—and a closing roundup Saturday evening provided the opportunity for everyone to display their creations.

Nights were given over to delicious meals shared in the Ranch's dining room with its expansive views and relaxed ambiance; extended cocktail hours, thanks to Padgett Printing's Becky Spillane who generously hosted the Hospitality Suite (in snakeskin pants no less); dancing under the stars to live music—highlights were Joel Nakamura and Andrea Bond's polished and nuanced two-stepping and San Antonio-based band Two Tons of Steel's rousing performance.

Remember summer camp? (I only got to go once. There was a bat in my cabin, I made an agate necklace and obviously didn't write home often enough, because I never got to go again.) Design Ranch is a grown-up version. Instead of counselors you get instructors who are principals of top design shops and award-winning illustrators and photographers.

English, an AIGA national board member, explained: "I've been going to conferences for seventeen years, from the Design Management Institutes shindig on Martha's Vineyard, to ICOGRADA's Montréal gig, to Tijuana's first international affair, and Guatemala's first national design conference. I have found that intimacy, locale and quality make for memorable experiences. Design Ranch is a private party, if you will, and everyone is invited." Conferences are often political, fraught with different factions of philosophy, approach and æsthetics.

At Design Ranch, everyone mingled and appeared to have an equally good time. Groups of people danced and talked until early morning, sharing stories and making friends. The smaller regional AIGA conferences—in Austin, Minneapolis, Seattle, San Diego and other cities—offer a counterpoint to an emotionally and intellectually challenging conference like the AIGA National Design Conference in Washington, DC [look for a conference review in the November 2002 *Design Annual*]. Unfortunately, as a result of continuing difficult business conditions, attendance was down by around one-third this year. As Bond wrote in the conference program, "The past year has been one helluva ride."

Yes, it has, but as Bond explained, "Design Ranch is about reconnecting to our work and to each other in very fundamental ways. It's about uncovering the passion that long ago propelled us into creative careers. It's about testing our artistic mettle and rediscovering our grit."

Grit indeed. It just goes to show that a combination of hand-based craft, toe-tapping music, great food and a gorgeous outdoor setting, can provide a much-needed respite from bottom-line analysis and deadlines—not to mention hotel ballrooms. It's also a good catalyst for reflection and change. My Stetson's off to AIGA Austin. The calendar is marked for Design Ranch 2003 (April 10–13) and my check's in the mail. ∎

One day at Design Ranch: James Victore rests on one of his workshop attendees' cardboard chairs and illustrators Joel Nakamura and Jennie Oppenheimer two-step under the stars. Photographs by Anne Telford.

Design Ranch poster. Laura Smith, illustrator; HeadGear: Creative, art direction/design; Jay Suhr/Andrea Bond, T3, writers.

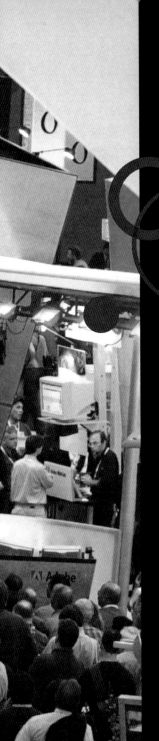

K3M Key3 Media Group PRESENTS

SEYBOLD

SEMINARS PUBLICATIONS SM

WHERE THE MEDIA TECHNOLOGY COMMUNITY MEETS

With so many creative communications tools and technologies in the marketplace, staying on top of industry innovations can be challenging for the publishing professional. Seybold Seminars delivers comprehensive education, a forum for in-depth technology discussions, and marketplace analysis—it has become the gathering place for buyers, sellers, and strategists around the world who all share the common goal of managing and delivering content across multiple media.

Through conferences, expositions, newsletters, and its Web site, Seybold Seminars provides an abundance of resources for publishing professionals to evaluate new technologies, debate standards, share successes and failures, and develop business strategies. Professionals can gain access to the latest in graphic design production tools, design and information architecture strategies, digital rights and asset management tactics, marketing personalization, and on-demand publishing opportunities.

Join us at our upcoming event, Seybold San Francisco, and be at the core of communications innovation and expertise.

Register online at
www.seyboldseminars.com
or call the Conference hotline at 888-886-8895

Upcoming Event: SEYBOLD SAN FRANCISCO | September 9–12, 2002, Moscone Center

 SEYBOLDSF
Design Build Communicate 2002

 SEYBOLDNY SEMINARS
Design Build Communicate 2003

 SEYBOLD PUBLICATIONS

 SEYBOLD REPORTS.COM

Coupon Code: 229   Priority Code: CAMG

 K3M Key3 Media Group

Book Reviews

Your Perfect Home-Based Studio
A Guide for Designers and Other Creative Professionals

By Poppy Evans
144 pages, hardcover, $29.99
Published by How Design Books
4700 E. Galbraith Road
Cincinnati, Ohio 45236
www.howdesign.com

A home-based design studio is a haven for constant disruptions. The temptations of snacking, watching TV and drinking beckon. Or the refrigerator calls for reorganization every time a creative block appears.

Distractions spell trouble for the self-employed designer according to Poppy Evans, former managing editor of *How* magazine. Evans has cataloged the list of pitfalls, as well as the advantages of the home-based, graphic design business in *Your Perfect Home-Based Studio*.

From startup costs and equipment needs to maintaining long-term clients, Evans details what every self-employed designer needs to know to become successful. Chapters are augmented with the examples of seventeen working professionals in their homes that include photos of the designer and their workspace, a floor plan, their equipment list and samples of their work.

This warm and cozy business manual is bright and accessible, but a book with this much information and inspiration would have benefited from better photography of the workspaces and better page color. The Popsicle hues defining each chapter compete with the busy case study layouts that include the designer's logo, a pull quote, running head, drop cap and a large folio.

Each section utilizes illustrations that, while colorful, are too generic to spark an interest in reading the chapter. Instead, more photos of well-lit workspaces would satisfy the voyeuristic appeal of walking into a designer's studio.

Aimed at recent graduates and newcomers to the field, *Your Perfect Home-Based Studio* is an upbeat resource book that is a thorough chronology of business development. The prospective self-employed designer is cautioned that it may take three to five years to find success in the business, but the upside is the dream that a designer can distract herself with her own work and that the personal freedom of working at home makes work a pleasure.

—Ruth Hagopian

Collapsible
The Genius of Space-Saving Design

By Per Mollerup
232 pages, hardcover, $29.95
Published by Chronicle Books
85 Second Street
San Francisco, California 94105
www.chroniclebooks.com

The Venus flytrap, the peacock and the snail all practice the same strategy of survival. They adjust their size to meet a practical need. They're collapsible.

They're also examples of hinging, fanning and expansion—three of the twelve mechanical principles of man-made collapsible objects. True collapsible designs function in both active and passive states and can change repeatedly.

The ingenuity of man-made collapsibles is confirmed by Per Mollerup, internationally-known Danish designer and director of Mollerup Designlab in Copenhagen. He has compiled hundreds of objects chosen for their design brilliance into an album produced to inspire creativity.

Like Dutch inventors G.H. and A.J. Vlutters, whose multistory building chute was inspired by stacking Dixie Cups, Mollerup hopes that viewing the pure originality from some of these objects will give birth to new invention.

Collapsible is an entertaining collection of ideas. Referring to the mechanics of size expansion in nature, Mollerup writes, "Size adjustment to meet functional requirements is a time-honoured principle in nature, too, as all real men and their happy mates will confirm."

His "real men" reference is curious, but Mollerup is frisky. His captions reflect a delight in these very clever, highly functional industrial designs that sometimes evoke a smile, like the body armor that collapses to become a metal belt or the fine Panama hat that will roll small enough to pass through a wedding ring.

Collapsible covers the concept, methods and applications of a significant design principle used in our daily life. Along with fun facts and history, it is of special interest to view oddities like the knapsack that unfolds to become a chair or the collapsible shower cubicle. Their unusual designs have the same purpose of all collapsibles; the economy of space and the economy of transportation.

—R.H.

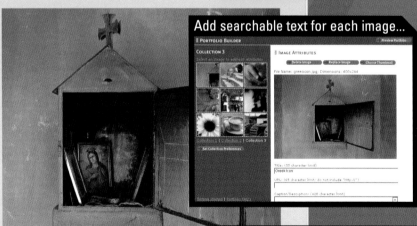
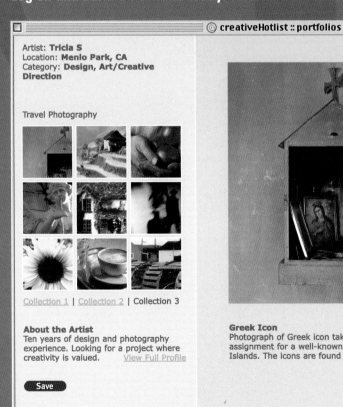

Book Reviews

Sensacional de Diseño Mexicano

By Juan Carlos Mena in collaboration with Oscar Reyes
240 pages, softcover, $35 includes CD-ROM

Trilce Ediciones, S.A.
Euler 152-403
Chapultapec Morales 11570
México, D.F.
www.trilce.com.mx

Princeton Architectural Press
37 E. 7th Street
New York, New York 10003
www.papress.com

Those who've traveled in México are most likely familiar with the common wall paintings and sign art that abounds there. In a country where the boundaries between artists, sign painters, muralists and graphic artists are less defined and literacy may vary, visual art in its most accessible form on the street, in wall paintings, signs and posters, takes on a greater importance in everyday life. *Sensacional de Diseño Mexicano* celebrates the color, texture and visual flavor of Mexican vernacular art. The book is nearly square in format and comprised of full-bleed images—mostly photographs of wall paintings, signs and lettering, but there are also a number of spreads showing posters, lettering and other printed ephemera.

Well paced and edited, *Sensacional* reveals wall paintings for the most basic business elevated in lively, expressive and personalized ways. These include caricatures of chickens, fish, crustaceans, plus colorful renderings of fruits, flowers, cakes, boldly-rendered appliances, bolts, tires, keys, welders, shoe repair, popular wrestling icons or smiling cartoon tooth figures for a dentist (guaranteed to dispel any fears). There is a kind of wonderful imperfection found in Mexican vernacular art that is honest—because it doesn't masquerade as something other than what it is. *Sensacional* reveals a wide range of styles and levels of technique—from a gang of salon signs including a sophisticated airbrush rendering of Penelope Cruz, to the simplest lettering or outline painting of a shoe for a cobbler. While some examples may appear technically crude or naïve, what may be considered lacking in terms of technique, though, is frequently made-up for in expressiveness and spirit—often with playful or offbeat humor. There are occasional amusing pop-cultural crossovers. For example, one wall painting shows the R2D2 *StarWars* droid with one arm holding a pizza. Another shows irreverent machismo humor integrating a painted form within its setting—a Pre-Colombian figure painted on a garage door with the chrome door handle appropriately positioned.

Trilce Ediciones's version of this book includes texts in Spanish by artist and designer Isaac Kerlow, designer Juan Carlos Mena and author Emiliano Pérez Cruz. Included is a lively multimedia CD-ROM produced by Mexico City-based Judo Media (**www.judomedia.com**) that perfectly complements the book. It contains QuickTime interviews (in Spanish) with *rótulistas* [sign painters] participating in a special Arte Modesta exhibition and letterpress printers in a shop specializing in wrestling posters, and also includes an interactive board game called *Taxis y Peseras* [taxis and buses]. This game and the interface (complete with traditional Mexican music soundtrack) of the CD-ROM incorporate many images found in the book. Also on the CD are seven digital fonts produced by Edgar A. Reyes as an homage to rótulistas, a collection of icons and desktop screens, plus a series of humorous business card templates.

This summer Princeton Architectural Press will release an English edition of this book (titled *Sensacional: Mexican Street Graphics*) with additional texts by musician/photographer David Byrne and art director/editor Steven Heller, but alas, without the CD-ROM.

Whether you obtain the original Trilce Ediciones version including the visually-rich CD-ROM—or the Princeton Architectural Press version, *Sensacional de Diseño Mexicano* is a brilliant visual survey of Mexican vernacular art that will inspire you and put a smile on your face with its clever surprises.

—MARK EASTMAN

Briefly noted:

Tomi Ungerer Erotoscope (Published by Taschen, 416 pages, hardcover, $70, **www.taschen.com**). Here the noted children's book illustrator (and one-time clock maker) has collected his erotic drawings into one hilarious, shocking and elucidating tome. Almost 200 drawings are published here for the first time—a nice 70th birthday present from Taschen. Alsatian artist Ungerer has published some 150 books over four decades "in his quest to open people's minds and abolish bigotry of all kinds," including many imaginative children's books. Of special note are early political pieces such as "Black power—white power," from the 1979 book *Politics*, showing two figures devouring each other, and two faceless men with rockets in their pants and the caption "Mine is Bigger, Ha! But mine is longer." Forbidden fruits are all the juicier for Ungerer who has an endless capacity for invention, turning bodies every which way with his fluid lines. Is his work erotic art or pornography? The answer must lie in the eye of the beholder, as Ungerer himself writes in his introduction, "What is the difference between erotic art and pornography? One trips here over the principle of relativity with its hordes of interpretations." The "Frogs and Flowers" section, depicting amorous frogs made me laugh out loud. The text, printed in English, German and French, conveys the artist's sense of humor and love of form; the extensive biography/bibliography section is a bonus.

—ANNE TELFORD

Technology

Photoshop, Painter & Illustrator Side-By-Side

By Wendy Crumpler
384 pages, softcover, $49.99
Published by Sybex Inc.
1151 Marina Village Parkway
Alameda, California 94501
www.sybex.com

Most of us who use a computer have mastered the application in which we most often work. But we know little, or have forgotten the essentials of other software. And we often find ourselves doing things in one application that might be best done in another.

To the rescue comes Wendy Crumpler, who as a production artist, illustrator and teacher knows her way around software. *Photoshop Painter & Illustrator Side-By-Side* is a software Rosetta Stone that translates methods and techniques from application to application. The book is handsomely illustrated with professional images that inform as well as inspire. In the back of the book, you'll find an artists' gallery with more excellent examples of computer art.

Ms. Crumpler writes like people speak, which is refreshing for a computer-related book where geek-speak seems to be the norm, and her editors even had the good sense not to excise her sense of humor and personal style. Even if you only use one of these applications, or need to get up to speed quickly on another, this book cuts to the chase providing concise, easy-to-understand methods and techniques.

There is something for everybody in this book including chapters on Layers, Masks and Channels, Color Basics, Paths and Shapes, Brushes, Type, the Web and more. Each chapter features a Side-By-Side table comparing functions and methods in each of the three applications (where appropriate). Each of the three applications is color-coded to make it easy to distinguish between illustrations. As new versions of these products are released, updated material will be posted on the publisher's (Sybex) Web site.

Photoshop Painter & Illustrator Side-By-Side is written for design professionals by a design professional. If you want

a better understanding of your software or want to expand your base of knowledge, this is the book for you.

—GARY W. PRIESTER

Design Invitational

By Deke McClelland
237 pages, softcover, $50 includes CD-ROM
An Adobe Press book published by Peachpit Press
1249 Eighth Street
Berkeley, California 94710
www.peachpit.com

Design Invitational takes readers beyond the "monkey see, monkey do" approach of most software "how-to" books. Instead, author Deke McClelland provides an "over-the-shoulder" look at how seven different artists at the top of their respective fields all approach the same project. The book is a pæan to Adobe software, since—no surprise—Adobe commissioned the project and published the results as an Adobe Press Book. There's plenty of step-by-step instruction here, along with the screengrabs, and the requisite work-in-progress snapshots. Readers will learn production tips, workarounds and specific techniques.

The seven artists include Craig Frazier, Michael Mabry, David Gare and Bart Marable, who cover the gamut of digital creation from illustration, photorealistic painting and typography to animation, Web site production and digital filmmaking. In all, it's a spectrum that puts Adobe products such as Illustrator, Photoshop, Premiere, After Effects, InDesign and InMotion through their paces (while avoiding offerings from competitors such as Flash, Final Cut Pro and Quark) and guarantees a wide readership for the book.

Along with their assignment—"Everywhere You look"—artists were given an Apple G4 Titanium PowerBook loaded with Adobe software, a digital camera and a top-of-the-line Epson inkjet printer. Each was asked to create a poster, a Web site, an animation or digital video according to their field of expertise. McClellan then observes their working methods, captures their thoughts as they talk about their methodology, and combines those with a step-by-step walkthrough of the project. The projects are broad enough to ensure that if you create digital graphics with a computer, there's a good chance you'll get something from this book, be it a trick or technique or just the inspiration you need to face the blank screen each day. Who knows, combine talent, inspiration and know-how with the right tools (like the ones Adobe plugs) and you might be invited to their next design invitational.

—SAM McMILLAN

REsources

Materials

Latin-American Vernacular Fonts

P22 Foundry recently released a new font package, under its International House of Fonts division, based on the work of José Guadalupe Posada, one of Mexico's greatest printmakers. The P22 Posada Set includes two Posada fonts that resemble late nineteenth century wood-types in both a regular and irregular, as lettering often appeared in Posada's illustrative works. A Posada Extras font is also included with 60 illustration icons and ornaments. Posada's illustration for broadsides and posters, using metal engraving and etching techniques, often depicted everyday events and people. His most well-known images, though, are of *calaveras* (skeletons). Posada's calaveras were not only used for the Day of the Dead celebration in Mexican culture, but also as a form of humorous caricature. The P22 Posada Set retails for $23.95. For more information, contact P22 at (800) 722-5080 or view samples and order online at **www.p22.com/ihof**

Designer Pablo Medina has been producing typefaces in the style of Latin-American vernacular sign lettering for a number of years. His faces such as Vitrina Script, a heavy script; and Cuba, a bold outline and shadowed sans commonly used by *rótulistas* (sign painters), have a lively personality all their own. His font 1st Avenue is based on the lettering of neon signs, but has a quality that is similar in feel to some of Posada's metal-engraved illustrations. For more information on these and other

Vitrina Script
ABCDEFGHIJK
abcdefghi0123456

P22 POSADA
ABCDEFabcde01234
ABCDEFabcde01234

CUBA
ABCDEFGH
01234567

Los Feliz
ABCDEFabcdef
ABCDEFabcdef
ABCDEFabcdef
ABCDEFabcdef

of Medina's fonts, call (800) 615-3533, e-mail info@cubanica.com or visit **www.cubanica.com**

Emigre, Inc. has recently released the new font family Los Feliz, produced by Cristian Schwartz and inspired by Latin-American vernacular sign lettering found in the Los Feliz area of Los Angeles. Schwartz incorporated some of the highly personalized nuances from his inspirational source and has produced a four-family font that has a unique personality, but is also a highly refined and functional typeface design. The Los Feliz package retails for $95. For more information, write Emigre Inc., 4475 D Street, Sacramento, California 95819, call (800) 944-9021 or you can view samples and order online at **www.emigre.com**

Special Introductory Pricing on Adobe OpenType Fonts

Adobe has recently completed conversion of the entire Adobe Type Library to OpenType format and is offering special introductory pricing on OpenType fonts through July 31. The OpenType Font format, developed jointly by Adobe and Microsoft over the last few years, allows more

characters and features in one compact, cross-platform compatible font file format. Previously Type 1 Postscript and TrueType format fonts were limited to about 256 characters. OpenType fonts that utilize Unicode, an international encoding standard, allow as many as 65,000 characters to be included in a typeface. Previously, an extensive text typeface family including small caps, expert character sets, ligatures, swashes, titling faces had to be broken up into separate typefaces making them difficult to use. OpenType format allows an entire family of styles and characters for one weight to be consolidated into a single font. This allows special characters and accents to be more easily implemented in programs with advanced features that make use of OpenType encoding such as Adobe InDesign 2.0. Ever get frustrated with your spell-checking function flagging every word you've applied ligatures to? With OpenType and OpenType enhanced programs, no more ligature spell-checking blues. OpenType's unicode encoding also makes it possible to spell-check in multiple languages and

visually select accented characters from pop-up palettes. For more information on these and the other benefits of OpenType fonts that will help you set better type and work more efficiently, plus listings of available fonts and online character set samples, visit the Adobe Web site (**www.adobe.com/type**) or call (800) 833-6687.

—Mark Eastman

Color Cue

You know that tool with the funny name, StudSensor? You run it down a wall and it lights up when it hits a stud, letting you hang pictures without putting multiple holes in the wall. Well, the PANTONE Color Cue has the same effect on color. You simply place this chic little machine on top of something whose color you want to match and…voilá! The easy-to-use, handheld spectro-colorimeter—preprogrammed with color data for the PANTONE MATCHING SYSTEM®—gives you the closest PANTONE Color match. Imagine the applications! Once you have a number, you can use their solid in RGB guide to gain a visual representation of the color. The Color Cue also gives you PANTONE Color ink formulas, CMYK, RGB, sRGB, HTML, Lab and PANTONE Hexachrome® values.

These tools can be used across many disciplines: Graphic designers can instantly determine a PANTONE Color and

REsources

its values for any type of reproduction, as well as proof color
from a desktop printer. Printers
can sample color and mix special
formulations to the closest
PANTONE Color. Retailers can
swiftly and easily identify and
communicate color across marketing materials, catalogs and
Web sites.

The Pantone Web site provides
testimonials that claim, among
other things, "It's the graphics
advantage that any product
development manager needs to
get ahead." It certainly can't hurt!

"We get a lot of inaccurate color
samples from our clients,"
explained Eddie Ellis, production
color analyst at Xerox Corp, who
consults to the graphic arts
industry. "We're using Color Cue
to measure inkjet proofs and take
a lot of the guesswork out of
color matching. It reduces two to
three hours of work down to a
few minutes."

The Pantone 430 C-colored tool
is 6" × 1½" wide × 1½" deep
and weighs only 3.4 ounces
without the battery (take it on
trips to the mall so everything
matches at home). It's not
inexpensive (regular price is
$349), but there's nothing out
there that does what it can.
Better lock your desk drawer
because everyone in
the office will want to
borrow it. Save $59
when you buy the
PANTONE Color Cue
together with the
PANTONE solid in RGB
guide ($109 sold
separately); special
bundle price is $399.
For more information,
or to order by phone,
call (888) PANTONE.

—Anne Telford

Mobile Workspace

While we may think of nomads
as wandering about with no real
residence, our shrinking global
society has taken on nomadic
characteristics, especially when
it comes to work. Traveling
from place to place, we've
adapted to life on the go. Our
PDAs, cell phones and other
technological gadgets have
become smaller and smaller in
an attempt to make our lives
more comfortable, efficient
and organized. Enter the Lapstation Pro by Intrigo. Touted as
the world's smallest desk, this
portable workstation was
designed by RKS Design with
the student, business professional and traveler in mind.
Weighing in at less than three
pounds, the Lapstation Pro
opens to a 20" × 11" anti-slip
work-surface *and* folds to a
1¼" profile. Smaller than the
average picnic bask...I mean
laptop when folded, the Lapstation Pro fits easily into any
briefcase, carry-on luggage or
backpack. It also has such
innovative features as ergonomic
curves for enhanced wrist support and shock-absorbing rubber
feet, and has been designed to
shield against computer heat and,
provides solid balance—anytime,

anywhere. As we travel through
life, our journey and the respon-
sibilities that come with it can
be achieved comfortably with
Intigro's Lapstation Pro. Afford-
ably priced at $49.95, check it out
at **www.intrigo.com**

Literature

Gilbert Paper presents
*Expert Opinions: Marketing
Materials: Fashion*, the fourth
publication in an ongoing series
where industry experts discuss
issues related to the design
community. Twelve fashion
authorities share viewpoints and
experiences on fashion design.
Reproduced on Voice, one of
Gilbert's textured papers, these
interactive discussions (Q&A
format) are accompanied by
examples of their work. The
demanding, ever-changing world
of style and fashion sit well
upon Gilbert's range of papers:
Realm Super Smooth, Esse
Smooth and Texture, Oxford,
and Gilclear. Speakers include:
Tanya Quick of Liska Design,
New York, for Lancôme &
Capezio; Ron Thompson of
Siquis Ltd., Baltimore, for
Woolrich & Bollman Hats; Peter
Arnell, The Arnell Group, New
York, for Donna Karan/DKNY;
Minda Gralnek, Target,
Minneapolis; Cathy Henszey,
Perry Ellis, New York; David
Edelstein and Lanny French,
Foundation, Seattle, for
Façonnable; Bill Blass & Tommy
Bahama; Holly Hunt, Great
Plains, Chicago; Kelly Friedl,
Titanium Design, Chicago, for
Ultimo, Bloomingdales and
Fitigues; Randy Elia and Peggy
Bennett, Bennett Elia Design,
Dallas, for Nieman Marcus; Patti
Okuno, The Limited, Columbus.

From black-and-white photography to illustration, subdued color
palettes to vibrant splashes of
color, Gilbert provides depth and
texture for annual reports, sta-
tionery programs and collateral
materials. To receive a copy
of *Expert Opinions: Marketing
Materials: Fashion*, log on to
www.gilbertpaper.com or
call (800) 445-7329.

**Showcase Illustration
25**, the two-volume source
book from American Showcase,
presents an abundance of artists
working in the areas of publishing, advertising, editorial,
collateral, packaging, etc. This
vast industry with its wide range
of styles is symbolized on the
covers of these two books: the
first features a more traditional
illustration from Dugald Stermer,
who, on the opening page,
discusses how collaboration has
changed during his long career;
Tom Nick Cocotos's illustration
on the second cover reveals one
of the many other directions
illustrators have ventured into,
and he talks of possibilities
opened up in collaborations and
the unexpected surprises of
working with collage. Artists'
Representatives make up the
first volume, more than 500
pages worth. The second volume is comprised of illustrators
and designers. The convenient
table of contents, index and
directory combine to make this
a useful resource for anyone in
the market for original illustration.
From one end of the spectrum
to the other, the pages inside
this 25th Anniversary source
book are a gateway of sorts,
providing just a glimpse into the
wide array of choices that exist.
For more information, check out
www.americanshowcase.com,

where you can Flip Through the Book; comb through the Advertiser's Alphabet, Illustrators' Representatives and Illustrators & Designers; Order a Copy; and get Rates & Specs. Don't forget to stop on by Theispot-Showcase site (**www.theispot .com**), the illustration Web site that encompasses just about everything going on in the field.

—Rebecca Bedrossian

Online

Stock

Customizable stock. That's the promise of Livestock's patent-pending image-customization process. In addition to the ability to customize a library of images, Livestock offers keyword searches, online ordering, account creation, large-image previews, a saveable lightbox and a purchase history. To learn more, call (888) 241-4413 or visit **www.livestockinc.com**

Virtual Reality travel. No lost luggage. Visit 51 of the largest cities in the world from your computer screen at **www.didik.com**. Photo editors, graphic artists and art directors who need street scenes and photographs of buildings will appreciate the library of photographs. The first city now online is New York, where tens of thousands of photographs have been compiled into a seamless view of every portion of Manhattan. Pack your bags and visit **www.nycinpictures.com**

Reprographic resource

A series of business strategies for reprographics professionals has just been compiled by the International Reprographic Association (IRgA). Business Strategies, the first volume in

the IRgA Industry Journal Series, is designed to equip reprographers with the tools to handle a wide range of financial and operational issues. Topics covered include development of effective sales and marketing, digital workflow design, business profitability and understanding and leveraging technology. For more information, send an e-mail to info@irga.com or go to **www.irga.com**

—Sam McMillan

Tools

QuarkXPress 5
Was it worth the wait?

QuarkXPress 5 has finally arrived with such features as Web publishing and XML support; redesigned features like an all-in-one Preferences box; and features that should have been included ages ago such as tables, layers, collect for output and context-sensitive menus.

Quark's new Media-Independent Publishing tools let users create Web pages, and eBooks using Quark's familiar set of tools. Support for XML provides a device for shuffling documents between print and electronic media.

Users can drag and drop elements from a Quark print document, or a thumbnail of an entire document, into a Quark Web document. Bitmap images (created in outside applications) can be used to create hyperlinked rollover buttons. Sophisticated forms can be created using the new Web Tools palette. Support for META tags, which are used by search engines to catalog Web sites, is also included. There is no FTP capability for uploading documents onto the Web, however.

Layers and Tables are new to

Quark 5. Layers are helpful for organizing complex documents and have the option of being invisible and/or non-printing. Tables can be created and modified with ease and individual cells can contain text or images. Cells can be combined, split, colored and resized. Visual indicators let you quickly identify on which layer an item resides and easily differentiate the various types of text and picture boxes in a Web document. The multiple Preferences menus have been combined into one convenient Preference Box. Context-sensitive menus have been added for increased workflow efficiency.

While these new additions are welcome, if you were hoping to see some breakthrough innovations such as those found in Adobe's InDesign 2.0, like transparency, soft shadows, adjustable Display performance and Multi-line composer, you might have to wait a while. Missing from Quark 5 is the ability to export PDF files without Acrobat Distiller and support of advanced features with OpenType fonts. The Web publishing features are good, but rather limited. Support for Flash SWF files and SVG images is absent, as is a carbonized version for Mac OS X (currently under development). And although there is a 1,500 page PDF manual, the online Help is very limited.

Because Quark owns the lion's share of the publishing software market, they probably don't think they have to be innovative or timely. Whether this is true or not, we'll have to wait and see.

For pricing and system requirements, visit **www.quark.com**

—Gary W. Priester

Online modules

Add more functionality to your Web site with easy-to-use e-commerce and database integration Modules from Xara Online. No programming required. Connectable e-mail, data management, form functions, automated product inquiry systems, personnel records and membership registration can all be added to a Web site without mastering programming languages or even HTML. For more information, visit **www.xaraonline.com**

QuarkXPress XTension

ShapeMaker from GLUON enables illustrators and designers to create shapes such as text columns, waves, polygons and spirals—quickly and easily using their new Shape Synthesizer technology. The ShapeMaker dialog interface features include previews, presets and controls for accuracy and precision. For more information, visit **www. gluon.com**

Photoshop plug-ins

Twenty new color threshold plug-ins for Photoshop users are available from Sapphire Innovations, Volume 6. The volume includes random grain, pencil, rain, newsprint and cut out plug-in effects. For more information, visit **www. sapphire-innovations.com**

REsources

Color management

Simple, networkable and scaleable color management solutions are available from X-RiteColor Master, a provider of quality assurance software for color and light measurement. Market applications include printing, plastics, coatings, paints, inks and textiles. X-RiteColor Master provides streamlined and accurate color capture, formulation, matching and management. Automated color calibration enables the creation of an accurate database. For more information, check out **www.xrite.com**

Print e-business solution

Printable 5.0, the newest release from Printable Technologies, offers a unique end-to-end solution that provides printing companies with everything needed to deliver branded online services to their customers. The platform incorporates capabilities to handle custom RFQ-driven negotiated ordering, as well as sophisticated and flexible media-catalog-based ordering, featuring custom-print, inventory picks and print-on-demand capabilities. For more information, visit **www.printable.com**

Education

Online courses

Take 'em naked. Online courses from Rochester Institute of Technology and IO Technologies include Becoming a Print Professional, Introduction to Getting It on the Web, Practical Color Management, Introduction to Digital Asset Management, Profitable Digital Solutions, Introduction to Document Imaging Work-flows and Introduction to Variable Data Imaging.

Online courses feature adaptive learning technology that enables students to customize their experience, targeting what they need to learn without wasting time. A free demonstration course is available at **www.training.rit.edu/online.html**

—S.M.

Calendar

July

University of California presents "What is Graphic Design (And Where is it Going?)" on Saturday, July 13, 10 a.m. to 4 p.m. at UC Berkeley Extension San Francisco Center, 55 Laguna Street, San Francisco; fee: $20. The panel of professional graphic designers will include Kate Godfrey, senior designer *PC World*; Markus Hogele, senior visual and interactive designer at frog design; and Gracie Artemis and Bruce Yelaska, instructors in UC Berkeley Extension's graphic design certificate program. Some topics the panel will tackle include: What are the roles and responsibilities of the graphic designer in the twenty-first century? As a field that both influences and responds to cultural trends, where is graphic design today? What does a successful graphic designer need to know in today's competitive marketplace, and how do they keep their skills current? To register, call (510) 642-4111 or register online at **www.unex.berkeley.edu/cat/034793.html**

August

The International Design Conference in Aspen (IDCA), the 52nd Conference, convenes in Colorado on August 21–24. "What matters now…Regroup, Reflect, Renew."

Join leaders in design, the arts, science and industry. Engage in dialogue with the 2002 program committee Walter Hood, Michael Rotondi, Lorraine Wild and other design board members: Paola Antonelli, Bran Ferren, Hella Jongerius, Mark Joseph, S. Joy Mountford, Gregg Pasquarelli, Billie Tsien and distinguished visionaries Ron Arad, Shigeru Ban, Mel Chin, Julie Bargmann, Sheila de Bretteville, Mary Jane Jacob and Bill Joy. For registration information, write IDCA, Registrar, P.O. Box 664, Aspen, Colorado 81612; call (800) 815-0059; fax (800) 815-0061; e-mail info@idca.org; or visit the Web at **www.idca.org**

September

The Portland Advertising Federation sponsors the thirteenth annual Portland Creative Conference September 12–14 at the Portland Center for the Performing Arts Center in downtown Portland, Oregon. This year's conference includes speaker presentations, panel discussions, sneak preview film screenings, an opening night kick-off celebration and a closing night wrap party. A complete schedule with speakers, panel topics and presenters is listed on the Web site at **www.creativeconference.org** or call (503) 525-4968.

The University & College Designers Association (UCDA) 32nd Annual Conference is set for September 14–17 at the Wyndham Hotel in Chicago, Illinois. Members invite you to network, create, refresh, collaborate, learn and explore. For information, contact UCDA, 153 Front Street, Smyrna, Tennessee 37167; call (615) 459-4559; fax (615) 459-5229; e-mail info@ucda.com; or visit the Web site **www.ucda.com**

The Association Typographique International (ATypI) Annual Conference is planned for September 19–22 in Rome, Italy. Members of ATypI include type designers and typographers, type foundries, graphic designers, writers, publishers, educators and students, manufacturers of typesetting equipment and typographic software, printers, advertising agencies, companies, professional organizations and associations interested in type and typography. For information, contact the Secretariat at ATypI, 10 Ridgeway Road, Redhill, Surrey RH1 6PH, United Kingdom; call +44 (0) 1737-780-150; fax +44 (0) 1737-780-160; e-mail atypi@sharonirving.co.uk; or check the Web site at **www.atypi.org**

AIGA/Minnesota presents its Design Camp September 27–29 at Ruttger's Bay Lake Lodge in Deerwood, Minnesota. The event draws 350-400 local and regional designers, photographers, writers, illustrators and other creative people. Speakers and workshops will be offered throughout the weekend. For information, contact AIGA/Minnesota, 275 Market Street, Suite 54, Minneapolis, Minnesota 55405; call (612) 339-6904; fax (612) 338-7981; or e-mail office@aigaminn.org; or visit the Web site **aigaminn.org**

—Jean A. Coyne

Copy must be received three months prior to the publication date. Please include a contact phone number and address.

strategies with other design-firm principals Get practical advice from experts in marketing and managing creative-service firms Learn
to fashion a useful client agreement Get tips for weathering an economic downturn Identify the traits of the "durable firm," and
how to make yours last a lifetime Create strategies ~~for~~ **HOW magazine and ReCourses, Inc.** ing your personal financial life
~~er~~ ways to use chemistry to **invite you to Scottsdale, AZ for the 3rd annual** ith clients Find out how to protect
firm when key employees leave Get expert advice for hiring, paying, motivating and keeping your staff Evaluate your firm's
~~performance~~ vs. industry benchmarks Experie **mind your** erican, Spanish and western cultures Tour the Sonoran
~~desert~~ in an open Jeep or Hummer Visit Frank Lloyd Wright's winter **own business** ~~of~~ architecture, Taliesin West Explore the Scottsdale
~~art~~ scene with a Thursday night ArtWalk Ride the trails **CONFERENCE** Treat yourself to a sunrise hot
~~balloon~~ flight over the desert Raft the Salt or Verde rivers Indulge in ~~hot-rock~~ massage or ~~cactus-flower~~ wrap at the Biltmore Spa

September 18-21, 2002
Arizona Biltmore Resort & Spa
Phoenix/Scottsdale

A business retreat for principals of design and creative-service agencies

WED SEPT. 18

4:00-7:00 pm	Registration
7:00-8:30 pm	**1. OPENING KEYNOTE** **The Five Critical Skills of a Successful Entrepreneur** *Dr. Ray Smilor*
8:30-10:30 pm	Opening Reception

Spend a few days working on your business instead of in it.

THUR SEPT. 19

	INSIDE Staffing, finances, strategy and other issues within your firm.	OUTSIDE Winning and working with clients.
8:00-8:50 am	**Breakfast Roundtables**	
9:00-10:20 am	**2. Creating Strategic Awareness in Your Staff** *Anne Haerle and Jeni Herberger*	**3. Your Branding Black Box** *Stuart H. Sanders*
10:40am-noon	**4. The Durable Firm — How Yours Can Last a Lifetime** *Richard H. Truitt*	**5. Helping Your Staff Interface Well with Clients** *Dave Wood*
noon-2:00 pm	Lunch on Your Own	
2:00-3:20 pm	**6. Managing Your Personal Financial Life** *David C. Baker*	**7. Chemistry Wins New Business** *Stuart H. Sanders*
3:40-5:00 pm	**8. Thriving Lean** *David C. Baker*	**9. Fashioning an Effective Client Agreement** *Michael C. Lasky*
5:00 pm	**Dinner on Your Own · Evening Free**	

FRI SEPT. 20

8:00-8:50 am	**Breakfast Roundtables**	
9:00-10:20 am	**10. Protecting Your Firm When Key Employees Leave** *Michael C. Lasky*	**11. Benchmarks to Measure Agency Performance** *Dave Wood*
10:40 am-noon	**12. The Durable Firm - How Yours Can Last a Lifetime** **(REPEAT)** *Richard H. Truitt*	
noon-2:00 pm	Lunch on Your Own	
2:00-3:20 pm	**13. Everything You Need to Know about Staffing Your Firm** *David C. Baker, Anne Haerle*	**14. Helping Your Staff Interface Well with Clients** **(REPEAT)** *Dave Wood*
3:40-5:00 pm		**15. Your Branding Black Box (REPEAT)** *Stuart H. Sanders*
8:30-11:30 pm	**Cocktail Reception**	

SAT SEPT. 21

8:00-8:50 am	Breakfast Roundtables
9:00-10:00 am	**16. Expert Panel Q&A** *Richard H. Truitt, Moderator*
10:15-11:30 am	**17. CLOSING KEYNOTE** **Making it Personal** *Bruce Kasanoff*

For complete session descriptions,
speaker bios and Scottsdale highlights, visit

www.MYOBconference.com

Your Arizona Biltmore retreat

Your home for the 2002 Mind Your Own Business Conference is the historic Arizona Biltmore Resort & Spa, situated at the foothills of Squaw Peak Mountain in Phoenix. Frank Lloyd Wright collaborated on the design of this extraordinary resort in the 1920s, and his influence is beautifully apparent throughout the property. Resort amenities include:

four restaurants
eight swimming pools
a 92-foot water slide and private cabanas
seven lighted tennis courts
two 18-hole championship golf courses
an 18-hole putting course
biking and hiking trails
croquet, lawn chess, table tennis and volleyball
Kids Kabana playground
a 22,000 square-foot spa and fitness complex

Conference attendees will receive a discounted room rate of $195 single/double, with one night's deposit due at time of reservation. The rate includes a daily Resort Fee, which covers admittance to the Biltmore Spa & Fitness Center, telephone charges, shuttle to the Biltmore Fashion Park shopping center, morning newspaper, use of putting course and self-parking. Suites or villas are also available at a 20% discount for Conference attendees.

To book your room, call **800-950-0086** and mention you're with the Mind Your Own Business Conference. These discounted rates are effective September 13-27, 2002. Reservation cutoff at the Biltmore is August 23, 2002. Reservations made after this date are on a space-available basis; however, the group rate still applies.

GETTING THERE
America West has discounted fares for MYOB Conference attendees flying into Phoenix Sky Harbor International Airport. To take advantage of these rates, call **Magellan Travel**, the official travel agency for the Conference, at **800-323-9230** and provide code number **6493**. Or, call America West directly at **800-548-7575**.

Renting a car? Avis is offering discounted rates for MYOB Conference attendees. Call **800-331-1600** and provide Avis Worldwide Discount (AWD) number **J991707**.

HOW TO REGISTER
Complete *both* sides of the form at right and fax or mail it as indicated. Or visit **www.MYOBconference.com** and register online. If you are registering multiple attendees from the same company, please submit a separate registration form for each person. Space is limited, so please register early. Registrations will be processed in the order they're received.

CANCELLATION POLICY
If you must cancel for any reason, please notify us in writing by August 19, 2002. Your registration fee will be refunded, less a $100 processing fee. No refunds will be made after this date. Substitutions may be made by phone, fax or email until September 4. After this date, all changes must be made on-site.

PHONE 800.436.8700 **FAX** 513.531.0798 **EMAIL** myobconference@fwpubs.com

---

2002 mind your own business CONFERENCE

REGISTRATION FORM

EARLY-BIRD DISCOUNT
Register before July 15 and save $200

1. PLEASE PRINT CLEARLY the following information as you'd like it to appear on your badge.

Name _____

Title _____

Company _____

Address _____

City _____ State _____

ZIP/PC _____ Country _____

Phone( ) _____ Fax( ) _____

Email | | | | | | | | | | | | | | | |

☐ You have my permission to include my name, company, city & state in the "Who's Attending" area of the Conference Web site.

2. CONFERENCE FEES

	Regular Rate	Early-Bird (before 7/15/02)	
☐ Single registration	$1,495	$1,295	$
☐ Additional registrant from same company (Must be received at same time as primary registrant.)	$1,395	$1,195	$
Guest Package: $250 Includes admission to all breakfasts and receptions. Applies to spouse, significant other or friend in a non-related industry. Name _____			$
CA0702		TOTAL	$

Method of Payment (Federal Tax ID #31-0205810)
Note: All payments must be made in U.S. currency drawn on a U.S. bank.

☐ Check or money order (payable to 2002 Mind Your Own Business Conference)

☐ MC ☐ VISA ☐ AMEX   Exp. _____

Card # _____

Signature _____

OVER ▷

3. SESSION CHOICES

WEDNESDAY, SEPTEMBER 18
- ☐ **7:00 - 8:30 PM** 1. OPENING KEYNOTE *Dr. Ray Smilor*
- ☐ **8:30 - 10:30 PM** Opening Reception

THURSDAY, SEPTEMBER 19
- ☐ **8:00 - 8:50 AM** Breakfast Roundtables

9:00 - 10:20 AM (choose one)
- ☐ 2. Creating Strategic Awareness in Your Staff
- ☐ 3. Your Branding Black Box

10:40 AM-NOON (choose one)
- ☐ 4. The Durable Firm — How Yours Can Last a Lifetime
- ☐ 5. Helping Your Staff Interface Well with Clients

2:00 - 3:20 PM (choose one)
- ☐ 6. Managing Your Personal Financial Life
- ☐ 7. Chemistry Wins New Business

3:40 - 5:00 PM (choose one)
- ☐ 8. Thriving Lean
- ☐ 9. Fashioning an Effective Client Agreement

FRIDAY, SEPTEMBER 20
- ☐ **8:00 - 8:50 AM** Breakfast Roundtables

9:00 - 10:20 AM (choose one)
- ☐ 10. Protecting Your Firm When Key Employees Leave
- ☐ 11. Benchmarks to Measure Agency Performance
  9:00 AM - NOON

10:40 AM-NOON
- ☐ 12. The Durable Firm - How Yours Can Last a Lifetime
  REPEAT

2:00 - 3:20 PM (choose one)
- ☐ 13. Everything You Need to Know About Staffing Your Firm
  2:00-5:00 PM
- ☐ 14. Helping Your Staff Interface Well with Clients **REPEAT**

3:40 - 5:00 PM
- ☐ 15. Your Branding Black Box **REPEAT**

- ☐ **8:30 - 11:30 PM** Cocktail Reception

SATURDAY, SEPTEMBER 21
- ☐ **8:00 - 8:50 AM** Breakfast Roundtables
- ☐ **9:00 - 10:00 AM** 16. Expert Panel Q&A
- ☐ **10:15 - 11:30 AM** 17. CLOSING KEYNOTE *Bruce Kasanoff*

☐ Check here to receive the **Mind Your Own Business Conference** email newsletter, with periodic updates on Conference events, sneak previews from speakers, and more.

☐ Check here if you have special needs that may require accommodation. A member of our staff will contact you to discuss your needs.

4. SUBMIT YOUR REGISTRATION

MAIL to:
Registration Dept.
2002 Mind Your Own Business Conference
4700 East Galbraith Road
Cincinnati OH 45236

FAX to:
513.531.0798
Attn: Natalie Davis

CALL:
Natalie Davis at
800.436.8700

SPEAKERS

This year's speaker lineup includes nine experts on business management, many of whom are former principals of design firms, ad agencies and marketing-communications firms. All now devote their careers to helping companies like yours grow and prosper.

David C. Baker *Nashville TN*
A management consultant and principal ReCourses, Inc., David is the co-foun and programming coordinator of the M Your Own Business Conference. A for marketing-communications firm princ turned business counselor, David has consul with hundreds of design firms, PR firms, agencies and other creative businesses. He e and publishes *Persuading*, a monthly newsle for principals of creative-service firms.

Anne Haerle *Kirkland WA*
Principal of DesignMatters, a consulting firm that helps designers and creative teams maximize their strategic value and effectiveness.

Jeni Herberger *Kirkland WA*
Founder of Big Fish Promotions, and a principal of the consulting firm DesignMatters.

Bruce Kasanoff *Westport CT*
An expert on personalization and customer relationships, and author of *Making It Personal: How To Profit from Personalization without Invading Privacy*.

Michael C. Lasky *New York NY*
Attorney and partner at Davis & Gilbert LLP, whose clients include PR, advertising and marketing-services agencies throughout the U.S.

Stuart H. Sanders *Richmond VA*
Founder of Sanders Consulting Group, a learning organization that helps marketing-communications companies and design firms grow and expand their reach.

Dr. Ray Smilor *La Jolla CA*
President of the Beyster Institute for Entrepreneurial Employee Ownership, and author of more than a dozen books on entrepreneurship and business development.

Richard H. Truitt *New York NY*
Principal of Truitt Partners LLC, a Connecticut-based communications consulting company, and a counselor to executives at communications firms throughout the world.

Dave Wood *Green Bay WI*
Founder of the Agency Management Roundtable, a consulting firm that works specifically with small advertising agencies, graphic design and PR firms.

"The single greatest benefit of attending the MYOB Conference was challenged. Having our beliefs, experiences and precepts abo industry, the clients and running a business addressed by experts field. I think for too long people in our industry just accept things t they are (i.e. late hours, high staff turnover, lack of client respect, work changed and/or compromised at the last minute). The Conf presented other options from people who have been there."

Lori
Principal, IdeaStudio

Paper donated by International Paper. Printed on Accent. Opaque Cover 65#. Accent is a registered trademark of IP.

Index to Illustrators

Index to Illustrators

Dana, Steven   84
Phone (914) 946-9727
sldana@earthlink.net
97 Sterling Avenue
White Plains, NY 10606

Davis, Paul   29, 144
Phone (212) 420-8789
paul@okdavis.com
14 E. 4th Street
New York, NY 10012

Day, Rob   7
Phone (317) 253-9000
r@robday.com
6095 Ralston Avenue
Indianapolis, IN 46220

Dearth, Gregory Montfort   110
Phone (937) 746-5970
gmdearth@gemair.com
4041 Beal Road
Franklin, OH 45005

Deboo, Cyrus   47
Phone +44 (208) 788-8167
cyrus.deboo@virgin.net
57 Ormonde Court
Upper Richmond Road
London SW15 6TP
United Kingdom

Decoster, Jeffrey   64, 113
Phone (415) 822-9430
mrjeff@sbcglobal.net
4104 24th Street, #367
San Francisco, CA 94114

de Sève, Peter   21
Phone (718) 398-8099
deseve@earthlink.net
25 Park Place
Brooklyn, NY 11217

Dewar, Nick   64
Represented by
Kate Larkworthy Artist Rep, Ltd.
Phone (914) 925-9672
kate@larkworthy.com
16 Rickbern Street
Rye, NY 10580

Dibley, Glin   37
Phone (714) 969-2405
20800 Beach Boulevard, #100
Huntington Beach, CA 92648

Dixon, Keith   135, 140, 144
Phone (323) 874-8242
keithdixon@sbcglobal.net
7349 Pacific View Drive
Los Angeles, CA 90068

Drescher, Henrik   37
Phone +852 (5) 9190-2551
Represented by
Reactor Art & Design
Phone (416) 703-1913 ext. 226
51 Camden Street
Toronto, Ontario M5V 1V2
Canada

DuBois, Gérard   55, 58, 84, 98
dubois@netaxis.ca
Represented by
Marlena Agency
Phone (609) 252-9405
marzena@bellatlantic.net
145 Witherspoon Street
Princeton, NJ 08542

Eberbach, Andrea   90
Phone (317) 253-0421
aeberbach@aol.com
5301 N. Delaware
Indianapolis, IN 46220
Represented by
Scott Hull Associates
Phone (937) 433-8383
68 E. Franklin Street
Dayton, OH 45459

Escobedo, Jacob   130
Phone (404) 758-7458
jakerry2@aol.com
1717 Shirley Street
Atlanta, GA 30310

Fancher, Lou   107
Phone (612) 377-8728
440 Sheridan Avenue S.
Minneapolis, MN 55405

Fanelli, Sara   21
Represented by
Riley Illustration
Phone (212) 989-8770
teresa@rileyillustration.com
155 W. 15th Street, #4C
New York, NY 10011

Faricy, Patrick   74
Phone (949) 858-8771
ratrik@cox.net
3 Stanford Court
Coto de Caza, CA 92679

Fedorova, Yvetta   90
Phone (212) 673-5363
yvetta.fedorova@verizon.net
640 Broadway, #3E
New York, NY 10012

Frazier, Craig   16, 71
Phone (415) 389-1475
studio@craigfrazier.com
90 Throckmorton Avenue, #28
Mill Valley, CA 94941

Freda, Anthony   79
Phone (212) 966-7330
anthonyf3@webtv.net
284 Mott Street, #5G
New York, NY 10012

Fuchs, Thomas   55
Phone (212) 904-1255
fuchsmail@aol.com
320 W. 37th Street, #9D
New York, NY 10018

Gall, Chris   11, 32
Phone (520) 299-4454
chris@chrisgall.com
4421 N. Camino del Santo
Tucson, AZ 85718

Glitschka, Von R.   7
Phone (503) 559-3020
von@glitschka.com
5165 Sycan Court SE
Salem, OR 97306

Grafe, Max   94
Represented by
Levy Creative
sari@levycreative.com
Phone (212) 687-6463
300 E. 46th Street, #8E
New York, NY 10017

Grahn, Geoffrey   84
Phone (310) 838-7824
geoffgrahn@earthlink.net
4054 Madison Avenue, #E
Culver City, CA 90232

Greif, Gene   76
Phone (212) 647-1286
genegreif@aol.com
114 W. 16th Street, #6E
New York, NY 10011

Grohmann, Helen-Lenio   107
Phone (212) 560-2535
leniogrohmann@yahoo.com
Prince Street Station
P.O. Box 184
New York, NY 10012

Guarnaccia, Steven   56
Phone (973) 746-9785
sguarnaccia@hotmail.com
31 Fairfield Street
Montclair, NJ 07042

Guy, Eddie   49
Phone (201) 251-7660
eddie.guy@verizon.net
309 Race Track Road
Hohokus, NJ 07423

Gwily, Ruth   56
Phone +972 (3) 635-9522
ruthgwily@hotmail.com
Shicun habanim 14
Kfar Azar 55905
Israel

Hahn, Michael   16
Phone +49 (406) 979-4432
michael@hahn-illustration.de
Hellbrookstrasse 61
22305 Hamburg
Germany

Harrington, Glenn   42
Phone (610) 294-8104
gharring@epix.net
54 Twin Leaf Road
Pipersville, PA 18947

Helton, Linda   125
Represented by
Marlena Agency
Phone (609) 252-9405
marzena@bellatlantic.net
145 Witherspoon Street
Princeton, NJ 08542

Henkel, Lars   30
Phone +49 (221) 420-4676
larshenkel@khm.de
Laurentiusstr.27
53123 Bonn
Germany

Hewgill, Jody   47, 51, 71
Phone (416) 924-4200
jody@jodyhewgill.com
260 Brunswick Avenue
Toronto, Ontario M5S 2M7
Canada

Holland, Brad   120
Phone (212) 226-3675
brad-holland@erols.com
96 Greene Street
New York, NY 10012

Hollenbach, David   51
Represented by
Frank Sturges
Phone (740) 369-9702
frank@sturgesreps.com
142 W. Winter Street
Delaware, OH 43015

Holley, Jason   47, 51, 61, 94, 96, 98, 107, 146
Phone (626) 836-7700
harpyinc@sprintmail.com
391 W. Grandview Avenue
Sierra Madre, CA 91024

Hooper, Hadley   56
Phone (303) 296-5583
hadleyhooper@earthlink.net
2111 W. 31st Avenue
Denver, CO 80211

Hughes, David   63
Phone +44 (161) 427-3852
43 Station Road
Marple, Cheshire SK6 6AJ
United Kingdom

Hundley, Sterling   64
Phone (804) 644-2034
sterling404@earthlink.net
1 N. 5th Street, #403
Richmond, VA 23219

Hussey, Tim   86
Phone (865) 525-5303
hussey_t@bellsouth.net
1023 Creek Road
Strawberry Plains, TN 37871

Huynh, Phung   73
Represented by
Frank Sturges
Phone (740) 369-9702
frank@sturgesreps.com
142 W. Winter Street
Delaware, OH 43015

Isip, Jordin   98, 118
Phone (718) 499-0985
jordin@jordinisip.com
536 5th Street, #2
Brooklyn, NY 11215

Jarrie, Martin   29, 52
Represented by
Marlena Agency
Phone (609) 252-9405
marzena@bellatlantic.net
145 Witherspoon Street
Princeton, NJ 08542

Jay, Alison   32
Phone (415) 537-4328
frontdesk@chroniclebooks.com
c/o Chronicle Books
85 Second Street, 6th Floor
San Francisco, CA 94105

Index to Illustrators

Savage, Stephen 56
Phone (718) 624-5435
stephen.savage@earthlink.net
93 Third Place, #3
Brooklyn, NY 11231

Schumaker, Ward 67
Phone (415) 648-8058
warddraw@best.com
630 Pennsylvania Avenue
San Francisco, CA 94107

Sealock, Rick 96
Phone (403) 276-5428
sealock@telusplanet.net
391 Regal Park NE
Calgary, Alberta T2E 0S6
Canada

Sherman, Whitney 68
Phone (410) 435-2095
ws@whitneysherman.com
5101 Whiteford Avenue
Baltimore, MD 21212

Sinclair, David Scott 103
Phone (617) 868-8887
sinc@sincstudio.com
99 Spring Street, #1
Cambridge, MA 02141

Skeen, Keith D. 109
Phone (608) 423-3020
kskeen@chorus.net
3228 Prairie Drive
Deerfield, WI 53531

Sloan, Michael 51
Phone (212) 253-2047
michaelsloan@earthlink.net
39 Linden Street
New Haven, CT 06511

So, Meilo 39
Represented by
The Artworks
Phone (212) 366-1893
sally@theartworksinc.com
455 W. 23rd Street, #8D
New York, NY 10011

Sorren, Joe 68, 79, 123,
  125, 127, 142
Phone (928) 214-9980
sparkle@infomagic.net
611 W. Aspen Avenue
Flagstaff, AZ 86001

Spiegelman, Art 58
Phone (212) 226-0146
spieg@learntech.com
95 Greene Street, #5B
New York, NY 10012

Stampatori, Riccardo
  117
Phone (519) 624-8202
rstampatori@rogers.com
60 Wadsworth Crescent
Cambridge, Ontario N1S 5A3
Canada

Stermer, Dugald 96
Phone (415) 777-0110
ds@dugaldstermer.com
600 The Embarcadero
San Francisco, CA 94107

Streeter, Katherine 67
Phone (212) 924-7966
dollhead@mindspring.com
17 Little W. 12th Street, #310
New York, NY 10014

Summers, Mark 32
Represented by
Richard Solomon Artist
  Representative
Phone (212) 223-9545
solomonart@aol.com
305 E. 50th Street, #1
New York, NY 10022

Sutherland, Marc 32
Phone (603) 742-4536
fatcan@aol.com
Olde Madbury Lane, #87
Dover, NH 03820

Taxali, Gary 7
Phone (416) 651-3737
gary@garytaxali.com
1 Wiltshire Avenue, #107
Toronto, Ontario M6N 2V7
Canada

Tillett, Anna 142
Phone (850) 476-6607
annabanana120@hotmail.
  com
7370 Beta Lane
Pensacola, FL 32504

Todd, Susan 123
Phone (416) 784-5313
stodd@interlog.com
146 Alameda Avenue
Toronto, Ontario M6C 3X2
Canada

Trenholm, Zach 98
Phone (415) 753-6020
zach@zachtrenholm.com
3649 Lawton Street, #642
San Francisco, CA 94122

Triplett, Gina 117
Represented by
Frank Sturges
Phone (740) 369-9702
frank@sturgesreps.com
142 W. Winter Street
Delaware, OH 43015

Trout, Julian 123
Phone (416) 588-8216
julian@juliantrout.com
385 College Street
Cobourg, Ontario K9A 3V5
Canada

Tsinganos, Jim 7
Phone +61 (02) 8308-3926
jim@tsinganos.com
2/254 Bondi Road
Bondi NSW 2026
Australia

Turgeon, Pol 135
Phone (514) 273-8329
polturgeon@netaxis.ca
5187 Jeanne-Mance, #3
Montréal, Québec H2V 4K2
Canada

Ueland, John 127
Phone (925) 449-9169
johnxjack@aol.com
1603 Frederick Michael Way
Livermore, CA 94550

Ulriksen, Mark 45
Phone (415) 387-0170
ulriksen@prodigy.net
841 Shrader Street
San Francisco, CA 94117

Unruh, Jack 83
Phone (214) 327-6211
jack@jackunruh.com
8138 Santa Clara Drive
Dallas, TX 75218

Valencius, Chris 8
Phone (617) 742-2549
chris@fortfranklin.com
11 Grove Street, #3
Boston, MA 02114

Ventura, Andrea 40
Phone (718) 349-3131
andreaventura@earthlink.net
346 Leonard Street
Brooklyn, NY 11211
Represented by
Richard Solomon Artist
  Representative
Phone (212) 223-9545
solomonart@aol.com
305 E. 50th Street
New York, NY 10022

Ventura, Marco 107
Represented by
The Artworks
Phone (212) 366-1893
sally@theartworksinc.com
455 W. 23rd Street, #8D
New York, NY 10011

Vitale, Stefano 142
Phone (516) 922-7130
stefanovitale@aol.com
49 Sandy Hill Road
Oyster Bay Cove, NY 11771

von Buhler, Cynthia 7
cynthia@drawbridge.com
Represented by
Lindgren & Smith
Phone (212) 397-7330
250 W. 57th Street
New York, NY 10107

Watson, Esther Pearl
  133
Phone (518) 392-9263
funchicken@earthlink.net
1772 Route 21
Valatie, NY 12184
Represented by
Jan Collier
Phone (415) 383-9026

Wearing, Paul 114
Phone +44 (207) 481-4653
paulwearing@illustrator.
  demon.co.uk
PW Art Limited, Unit B4,
Metropolitan Wharf
Wapping Wall,
  London E1W 3SS
United Kingdom

Weiner, Jonathan 49
Represented by
Levy Creative Management
Phone (212) 687-6463
sari@levycreative.com
300 E. 46th Street, #8E
New York, NY 10017

Wells, Leigh 89, 146
Phone (212) 627-8518
leigh@leighwells.com
17 Little W. 12th Street, #310
New York, NY 10014

Whadcock, Ian 49
Represented by
Eastwing Illustration Agency
Phone +44 (207) 613-558098
Columbia Road
London E27 QB
United Kingdom

White, Eric 127
Phone (718) 369-1167
e@ewhite.com
123 Seventh Avenue, #230
Brooklyn, NY 11215

Wiggins, Mick 90
Phone (510) 524-3076
mwiggins@dnai.com
1103 Amador Avenue
Berkeley, CA 94707

Wilkins, Sarah 47
Represented by
Riley Illustration
Phone (212) 989-8770
info@rileyillustration.com
155 W. 15th Street, #4C
New York, NY 10011

Wilson, Gahan 83
Phone (631) 725-1491
25 Henry Street
Sag Harbor, NY 11963

Wilton, Nicholas 24,
  103, 110, 118, 128
Phone (415) 488-4710
nick@zocolo.com
220 Alta Avenue
Lagunitas, CA 94938
Represented by
Jan Collier
Collier Represents
Phone (415) 383-9026

Wood, Ashley 37
ash@ashleywood.com

Woods, Noah 110
Phone (310) 659-0259
noahwoods@mindspring.com
927 Westbourne Drive
Los Angeles, CA 90069

Yang, James 110
Phone (212) 987-5917
james@jamesyang.com
225 E. 95th Street, #25J
New York, NY 10128

Yeo, Brad 94
Phone (403) 237-5553
yeob@cadvision.com
602 8th Avenue NE
Calgary, Alberta T2E 0R6
Canada

Zeltner, Tim 68
Phone (416) 588-8115
info@i2iart.com
27 Marchmount Road
Toronto, Ontario M6G 2A8
Canada

Editor's Note
Every effort has been made
to ensure that the credits
comply with information
supplied to us. If, for any
reason, a misspelling,
omission or other error has
occurred, notify us within 30
days and we will be able to
issue corrected award
certificates.

Index to Individuals and Firms Represented in the 43rd Illustration Annual

Index to Individuals and Firms Represented in the 43rd Illustration Annual

Editor's Note

Every effort has been made to ensure that the credits comply with information supplied to us. If, for any reason, a misspelling, omission or other error has occurred, notify us within 30 days and we will be able to issue corrected award certificates.

Directory

Featured in this issue

Fresh

delux design associates
19 Marble Avenue, Suite 4
Burlington, VT 05401
(802) 862-8355
(802) 862-8362 fax
www.deluxdesign.com

Charles Glaubitz
205 W. Date Street
San Diego, CA 92101
U.S.: (610) 233-9633, ext. 109
México: +52 (664) 674 47 98
www.mrglaubitz.com
**www.altpick.com/
   mrglaubitz**

Kenny Johnson
400 E. 17th Street
Kansas City, MO 64108
(816) 471-1200
(816) 474-4744 fax
kenny.johnson@kennyj.com
www.kennyj.com

Columns

Design Issues

Roger Whitehouse
Whitehouse & Company
18 E. 16th Street, 7th Floor
New York, NY 10003
(212) 206-1080
whitehouse@netstep.net

Design Culture

John Paul Caponigro
73 Cross Road
Cushing, ME 04563
(207) 354-0578

Freelance

Barbara Gordon
Barbara Gordon
   Associates Ltd.
165 E. 32nd Street
New York, NY 10010
(212) 686-3514
(212) 532-4302 fax

Legal Affairs

Tad Crawford
Allworth Press
10 E. 23rd Street
New York, NY 10010
(212) 777-8395
crawford@allworth.com
www.allworth.com

Advertising

Luke Sullivan
WestWayne
1170 Peachtree Street,
   15th floor
Atlanta, GA 30309
(404) 347-8730
(404) 347-8907 fax
lsullivan@westwayne.com

Business

Ruth Hagopian
coma2000@aol.com

Trillium Press
91 Park Lane
Brisbane, CA 94005
(415) 468-8166
Info@trilliumprints.com
www.trilliumprints.com

Opinion/ Commentary

Dugald Stermer
600 The Embarcadero
San Francisco, CA 94107
(415) 777-0110
ds@dugaldstermer.com
www.dugaldstermer.com

Conference Review

AIGA Austin Design Ranch
PMB 549
815-A Brazos
Austin, TX 78701
(512) 374-4456
www.aigaaustin.org

REsources

Sam McMillan
sam1067@pacbell.net

Gary W. Priester
The Black Point Group
47 Tejon Cañon Road
Placitas, NM 87043
(505) 867-5832
garypriester@earthlink.net

How to Reach CA

Communication Arts
110 Constitution Drive
Menlo Park, CA 94025-1107
(650) 326-6040
(650) 326-1648 fax
www.commarts.com

e-mail: ca@commarts.com
advertising@commarts.com
clubs@commarts.com
dealer@commarts.com
editorial@commarts.com
letters@commarts.com
shows@commarts.com
subscription@commarts.com

Subscriptions

(800) 688-1971 inside U.S.
   and Canada.
(850) 682-7644 outside the
   U.S. and Canada.
subscription@commarts.com
Order online at:
www.commarts.com

Subscription Rates:

U.S.: one year $53;
two years $99.
Canada: one year $70 (U.S.);
two years $129.
Includes GST #127848620.
International: one year $110
(U.S.); two years $199.

Send change of address notification at least 45 days prior to effective date, include both old label and new address.

Send subscription orders and address changes to:
Communication Arts
P.O. Box 51785
Boulder, CO 80322-1785

Retail Sales

To carry Communication Arts in your store, call Gloria Rosario at (650) 326-6040 or e-mail: dealer@commarts.com

Single Issues

January/February	$ 8
March/April	$ 8
May/June	$ 8
July Illustration Annual	$16
August Photography Annual	$16
September/October Interactive Annual	$16
November Design Annual	$24
December Advertising Annual	$24

California residents, add 8.25% sales tax. Canadian residents, add 7% GST. All orders: For shipping, add $4 (U.S.) per issue, all other countries add $5 (U.S.) per issue.

No responsibility will be assumed for unsolicited editorial contributions. Manuscripts or other material should be accompanied by a self-addressed stamped envelope adequate to return material or your Federal Express number.

All press releases must be received at least three months prior to the issue release date to be considered for publication. Due to the volume of press releases we receive, we are unable to respond to each one individually. Please don't call to see if we have received yours. Please send press releases on Books, Materials, Literature and Technology, including Conferences to Anne Telford, managing editor. Send press releases on Clubs, Conferences, Seminars, new hires, promotions, address changes, etc., to Jean Coyne, executive editor. While we don't have a column that deals specifically with new hires, promotions and address changes, we do want to be notified to update our database.

Hardware

Apple Macintosh G4 Power PC computers running on Ethernet network; Apple, Sony Trinitron and Super-Match monitors; Agfa Duoscan 2000XL, Agfa Arcus II, HP Scanjet 4C/T scanners; HP LaserJet 8100 laser printer.

Software

QuarkXPress for page layout, Microsoft Word for word processing and Adobe Photoshop for scanning and positioning images.

Typography

Adobe Garamond
Adobe Garamond Expert
   (Robert Slimbach)
Linotype Univers
   (Adrian Frutiger/
   Linotype staff)

Printer

Anderson Lithograph
3217 S. Garfield Avenue
Los Angeles, CA 90040
(323) 727-7767
(323) 722-2328 fax

Paper

Appleton Papers
Utopia Two
   Gloss 80 lb. cover
   Gloss 80 lb. text

Mailing Carton

Quality Container Company
1420 N. Claremont
   Boulevard, #205A
Claremont, CA 91711
(909) 482-1850
(909) 482-1853 fax

Prepress

Consultex
990 San Antonio Road
Palo Alto, CA 94306
(650) 322-3999
(650) 322-3998 fax
output@consultex.com

Image Color and
   Filmwork, Inc.
2161 O'Toole Avenue, Suite F
San Jose, CA 95131
(408) 954-8580
(408) 954-1477 fax

Prepress Assembly, Inc.
80 Langton Street
San Francisco, CA 94103
(415) 621-8970
(415) 621-3105 fax

Order Back Issues Online at: www.commarts.com

May/June 2002

March/April 2002
Illustration © Cynthia von Buhler

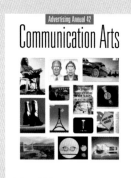

January/February 2002
Photograph © Dominique Malaterre, Tilt

December 2001
Advertising Annual

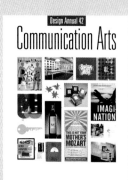

November 2001
Design Annual

September/October 2001
Illustration © Anja Kroencke

August 2001 Photography Annual
Photograph © Mark Richards

July 2001 Illustration Annual
Illustration © Douglas Fraser

May/June 2001
Illustration © Mark Ryden

December 2000
Advertising Annual

You can order back issues of *Communication Arts* by logging on to our Web site, **www.commarts.com**, by phone at (800) 258-9111 in the U.S. and Canada or (650) 326-6040 in all other countries, or by mail using the form at right. All orders must be accompanied with payment. For shipping within the U.S., please add $4 (U.S.) per issue. All other countries, please add $5 (U.S.) per issue. California residents, please add 8.25% sales tax. Canadian residents, please add 7% GST. Allow up to three weeks to receive your order. International orders 4–6 weeks. All back issues are subject to availability, we will refund your money on any issues that may have sold-out.

July 1994 $16
1994 Illustration Annual; Technology Feature: MicroColor

August 1996 $16
1996 Photography Annual; Technology Feature: Photographer's Web Sites

January/February 1997 $8
Alexander Gelman; RJ Muna; Roche Macaulay & Partners; Janet Woolley; Color Predictions; Great Ideas on Limited Budgets; Éco; Exhibit; Index to Volume 38; Technology Feature: ACD Conference: Design for the Internet

March/April 1997 $8
Mary Ellen Mark; Big Bang Idea Engineering; Specialty Beer Label Design; René Milot; Clients & Designers: Des Moines Metropolitan Waste Authority and Pattee Design; Éco; Exhibit; German Advertising; Technology Feature: Corbis Corporation

July 1997 $16
1997 Illustration Annual; Technology Feature: Nancy Stahl

August 1997 $16
1997 Photography Annual; Technology Feature: Stock Photography on Web

November 1997 $24
1997 Design Annual; Technology Feature: Digital Type Web Sites

March/April 1998 $8
Grafik Communications Ltd.; Joe Sorren; Butler, Shine & Stern; KDSP Design Group; Rodney Smith; Typographic Voices; Éco; The Richard and Jean Coyne Family Foundation; Exhibit; Technology Feature: Pittard Sullivan

May/June 1998 $8
Bianco & Cucco; Peter de Sève; Wolfgang Weingart; Hunt Adkins; Frans Lanting; Luba Lukova & James Victore; Great Ideas on Limited Budgets; Éco; 1998 Salary Survey; Exhibit; Technology Feature: Austin, Texas, Multimedia Scene

July 1998 $16
1998 Illustration Annual; Technology Feature: M.A.D.

August 1998 $16
1998 Photography Annual; Technology Feature: Digital Camera Review

December 1998 $24
1998 Advertising Annual; Technology Feature: Red Sky Interactive.

January/February 1999 $8
The Leonhardt Group; Natalie Ascencios; Color Predictions; Christine Alicino; Kan & Lau Design Consultants; Palmer Jarvis DDB; Broadcast Design Association; Éco; Exhibit; Index to Volume 40; Type Designer Jim Parkinson; Technology Feature: Art Technology Group

March/April 1999 $8
Communication Arts 40th anniversary issue; Nine Ways to Improve an Ad; Timeline; Stock Trademarks; Clients and Designers: Doug Oliver/Jim Cross/Mike Weymouth/Peter Harrison and Les Day, Northrop Coporation's Annual Report from 1961 to 1997; David's Lemonade; Éco; Paul Rand; Doyle Dane Bernbach; Pioneers; Technology Feature: Paul Saffo

July 2000 $16
2000 Illustration Annual; Technology Feature: Pixar Animation Studios

August 2000 $16
2000 Photography Annual; Technology Feature: James Porto

December 2000 $24
2000 Advertising Annual; Technology Feature: OgilvyInteractive

January/February 2001 $8
Grant Design Collaborative; Nanette Biers; Singapore Advertising; Kwaku Alston; Album Cover design; Pioneers: Helmut Krone; Color Predictions; Éco; Exhibit; Index to Volume 41; Technology Feature: THUNKdesign

March/April 2001 $8
Planet Propaganda; Stephen Wilkes; West & Vaughan; Imaginary Forces; Barbara Nessim; Exhibit; Éco; ¡Viva! Diseño en México; Fresh: Imagewerks; Open; Nichole Sloan

May/June 2001 $8
Ralph Appelbaum Associates Incorporated; Mark Ryden; Marc Sixdeniers; Abbott Mead Vickers BBDO; Deborah Jones; Tsunami of Change: a new wave of Japanese design; Exhibit; Éco; Great Ideas on Limited Budgets; Pioneers: Otto Storch; Fresh: Janusz Kaminski; Carbon¹⁴; Slavimir Stojanović

July 2001 $16
2001 Illustration Annual; Fresh: Stereotype; Liz Lomax; Graham Rounthwaite

August 2001 $16
2001 Photography Annual; Fresh: Steve Ditko; Shelly Reese; 300FeetOut

September/October 2001 $16
Viva Dolan; Lars Toplemann; BVK McDonald; Anja Kroencke; Exhibit; Éco; Interactive Design Annual 7 + CD-ROM; Fresh: Corey Sandelius; Piper Design Co.; Viktor Koen

November 2001 $24
2001 Design Annual; Fresh: Michelle Hinebrook; Olive; Amanda Friedman

December 2001 $24
2001 Advertising Annual; Fresh: Taco Zuidema; Renato Brito Castellani; Daniel Furon

January/February 2002 $8
Mires; Dominique Malaterre, Tilt; hillmancurtis, inc.; Chris Gall; Core; The Colorado International Invitational Poster Exhibition; Éco; Exhibit; Pioneers: Armando Testa; Fresh: Motion Theory, Molly Zakrajsek, Kevin Twomey; Index to Volume 42

March/April 2002 $8
Werner Design Werks; John Offenbach; Department 3; Cynthia von Buhler; Rick Colby; Merchandising Designers; Éco; Exhibit; Fresh: Public, Irit Hayton Studio, Smári

May/June 2002 $8
WPa; Jack Molloy & Elvis Swift; Sawyer Riley Compton; Martin Schoeller; Great Ideas on Limited Budgets; Salary Survey; Pioneers: Nicolas Sidjakov; Éco; Peter de Sève and *Ice Age*; Exhibit; Fresh: Michelle Thompson, Zinzell, John Eder

BUSINESS REPLY MAIL
FIRST-CLASS MAIL   PERMIT NO. 103   MENLO PARK CA

POSTAGE WILL BE PAID BY ADDRESSEE

NO POSTAGE
NECESSARY IF
MAILED IN THE
UNITED STATES

Communication Arts

110 CONSTITUTION DRIVE
MENLO PARK CA 94025-9359

FOLD ALONG THIS LINE

PLEASE TAPE CLOSED [NO STAPLES PLEASE]